Proving You're Qualified

/

Proving You're Qualified:

Strategies for Competent People without College Degrees

Charles D. Hayes

Autodidactic Press

Copyright © 1995 by Charles D. Hayes

Cover design and illustration by Lightbourne Images © 1995. Book design and typography by Synergistic Data Systems.

Library of Congress Catalog No. 94-96544
Publisher's Cataloging in Publication
(Prepared by Quality Books Inc.)

Hayes, Charles D.
Proving you're qualified : strategies for competent people without
    college degrees / Charles D. Hayes. — 1st ed.
    p. cm.
Includes bibliographical references and index.
Preassigned LCCN: 94-96544
ISBN 0-9621979-1-2

1. Professional education. 2. Career development.
3. Self-culture. I. Title
LC1059.H39 1995   378.013
                                         QBI94-21220

Printed in the United States of America

10 9 8 7 6 5 4 3 2 1

First Edition

Autodidactic Press
P.O. Box 872749
Wasilla, Alaska 99687

Contents

16.95

Acknowledgments

W riting a book is never a solitary effort. I am indebted to a number of people who may be totally unaware of how their ideas or actions have made a contribution. Conversations, probably long-forgotten, with Jeff Andersen, John Parker, Paul Peterson, James Kley, and Greg Taylor helped shape this text. I am grateful for the special assistance provided by my sister, Cheryl Hayes Wright, and for the following people who read and commented on this work in manuscript form: Jane Baldwin, James R. Fisher Jr., Randy Presley, and Bob Talbott. And finally a special thank you to my editor, LuAnne Dowling, who does for my ability to communicate what water does for plants.

I would also like to acknowledge Academic Press and Randall Collins for allowing me to quote extensively from *The Credential Society*.

Introduction

*There are many dull-witted people working in fields and facto-
ries, but there are also many dull-witted people practicing medicine, teaching school, managing corporations, and working as
sociologists. The assumption that a man and his labor are of the
same intellectual or cultural level is founded in the arrogance of
the observer.*

—Earl Shorris

E ach day thousands of experienced, competent people in America are denied job opportunities and well-deserved promotions
because of a lack of formal credentials. Often the credential requirements are arbitrary, having nothing whatsoever to do with the job
in question. The result is that organizations lose added value and
the individuals involved lose money, prestige, and fulfillment. Nothing in the workplace is more frustrating than being asked to fill a
job temporarily until someone more "qualified" can be found to fill
it permanently. Inevitably, once the "qualified" candidate is found,
the fill-in will be asked to provide the necessary training and orientation. This kind of scenario is one of many that give rise to a morale
problem permeating the whole structure of the American work
force.

The general sense of fairness that should prevail is undermined
by a tacit belief that one's effort will not be rewarded in proportion
to the effort expended. This problem derives from our reliance on
a procedure for judging competence and merit that is fundamentally
flawed and inherently inefficient—a system that can be as destructive to those who appear to benefit as it is as to those who are
prevented from advancement. For decades we have hired and promoted people based on what we assumed was merit, and yet we
have remained indifferent to the reality of how merit plays out in
actual practice.

Credentials are an attempt to offer proof that we can do what we
say we can do. I say *attempt* because anyone with experience in the
workplace can attest to the fact that credentials cannot be counted
on as proof of competence. Establishing credentials should be no
more complicated than proving competence. But proof of competence should consist of more than evidence of school attendance,

effective use of short-term memory, and an ability to adapt to a classroom environment.

In the course of promoting my previous book, *Self-University*, I have been asked more questions about the subjects of qualification and promotion than any other aspect of self-education. The idea to write this book occurred to me while doing radio shows to promote *Self-University*. Every time I spoke about the problems of credentialing the telephone switchboards lit up. The callers' anger and extreme frustration were immediately apparent. Since then, I have continued to study the problems associated with credentials and promotions, observing the hiring and promotion process from close up and at a distance. Reflection on my own experience as an employee and as a supervisor has provided insight into problems that are seldom discussed or written about.

I have more than 30 years of work experience in varying types of employment settings. I've been a U.S. Marine, a police officer, a factory worker, a salesman, and a publisher, and I have spent more than a decade and a half working for a major oil company. In all of my experience I have never been able to discern definitive differences traceable to levels of formal education among people performing similar jobs. I have worked with and for people with impressive degrees who were, without question, incompetent. I have worked with and for people with little formal education who were exemplary employees whom you would never suspect lacked any knowledge worth having. On numerous occasions I have seen people with no experience perform tasks better on the first attempt than people who had been performing the same task for years and had spent considerable time studying their field.

I have witnessed hundreds of conflicts over which employees should be promoted and which credentials should be required for a given job. I am convinced that our system of qualification does as much harm as it does good. Competence should be more important than credentials, and knowledge, *no matter how it is obtained*, should count more than proof of attendance in what are often ridiculous qualifying exercises. For the sake of businesses, individuals, and learning institutions, evidence of competence should be possible through the demonstration of a person's effort, not limited to what it is "thought" the person knows.

The ability to shoot straight can be quickly demonstrated, whereas a certificate that says you can shoot straight may be counterfeit. Why, then, does it make sense to accept certificates instead of target practice when choosing shooters? Why are people known to be expert marksmen asked to step aside to make way for people who have shooting certificates but are unable to hit the broad side of a barn? Thank goodness we do not do this with airline pilots. Airline pilots have to prove they know what they are doing under the direct scrutiny of others who have already proved their own competence: would that such *demonstrated ability* carried more weight in other arenas. Take instruction, for example. I have watched enthusiastic individuals with no formal credentials conduct training sessions and hold audiences spellbound. Their high interest, coupled with hands-on experience, engenders a genuine enthusiasm for learning among the trainees. In contrast, I have observed people with graduate degrees in teaching whose training exercises were so dull as to quash anyone's curiosity about the subject matter.[1]

My interest in the mechanics of merit and promotion over the years has spawned some ideas about work that many people will find politically incorrect. For one, if a job is worth doing, it is worth a living wage. When I was 21 years old, I would have simply brushed aside the problem of impoverishingly low wages as a question of economics and achievement. But, at 50+, have learned that economics is only a euphemism for politics. So, to a large degree (pun intended), is the whole process we call "qualification."

It has been my observation that few Americans respect what they do not understand. Thus, it makes a lot of sense to air these issues thoroughly. I must warn you however, that understanding credentialism may increase your level of anxiety, even if you are able to rise above it. Clearly, seeing the absurdity in a system which most people take as self-evident can be very upsetting. The positive side of adding a bit of reality and objectivity to your perspective is that sometimes you can win skirmishes in this battle. At the very least, it's worth a great deal to realize that you haven't been crazy all these years. Much of the groundwork necessary to successfully challenge arbitrary credentialing policies can be found in thoroughly understanding the senselessness of them. Once you can see that the emperor has no clothes, the methodology of how to prove this to others becomes clearer. The situation is easier to combat when you understand it better than anyone else, even if you have to defy what is accepted as common sense and conventional wisdom.

This book is idealistic in nature. I do not for a minute pretend otherwise, nor do I wish to whitewash my cynicism away completely—you may need some of it to temper your apprehension. My idealism springs from the simple but profound premise that the genuine value of human beings is neither dependent upon, nor is it discernable by, the positions they hold within economic hierarchies.

Throughout these pages you'll encounter arguments which seem to contradict each other. For example, on the one hand, I may suggest that if you have legitimate suitable experience, then educational credentials are not necessary. But, at the same time, I'll explain to you how to go about getting those credentials. I may suggest that formal education has little to do with workplace reality, but in the next sentence I will imply there is a direct connection. You'll think I'm talking out of both sides of my mouth, yet I know of no other way to be true to the title of *Proving You're Qualified* than to press both of these realities to the best of my ability. The process involves acknowledging both the reality of what is and what ought to be.

We are living in fast times. Politicians propose to reinvent government, and corporate leaders talk of reinventing business. It seems to me it would be even more meaningful and efficacious to reinvent the process we call qualification. A complete reexamination of that dynamic would eventually lead to better government through a greater democratization of opportunity. But, before we pursue such a trajectory toward the future, we must have a clearer examination of the present.

The first of the chapters that follow lays out our dilemma in three parts: common misguided expectations about merit and achievement, the stranglehold on knowledge which has resulted from such expectations, and a straightforward remedy designed to fulfill the original purpose of achieving merit. Chapter Two offers insight into just how formidable our hierarchical system has become and how the forces of technology and global economics are beginning to erode its foundation. The third chapter presents a critical discussion of management, the dynamics of promotional policies, and the amount of effort required to influence these practices. Chapter Four examines the nature of credentialing methods, and Chapter Five takes a closer look at the questions surrounding who is really qualified to do what. A list of choices and options to further develop your own approaches follows in the sixth chapter. Chapter Seven surveys the nature of change in the information age and revisits the subjects of organizations and management in that context. Chapter Eight pulls together the lessons of the first seven chapters and, under the rubric of Me, Inc., provides a structure for proving you are qualified. What becomes clear throughout is that effecting real change in the existing system involves upending long-held, emotion-laden beliefs. This can only take place from the bottom up, and it's our responsibility to make sure the need is not ignored.

This is not a book for rocket scientists and neurosurgeons, although a great many of them might do well to read it. This book is for the thousands of competent people in America who learned their jobs while doing them (certainly many scientists and surgeons qualify), but whose direct experience is valued less than the power of distant institutions. This book is intended to help you answer the question: "Should I go back to school?" Or, for those who are fresh out of school, this book may put into perspective what otherwise might take decades to learn. Most of all, this book is for those who have paid their dues through competent performance, but who are having difficulty proving it in the face of age-old, errant assumptions about the nature of qualifications. It will help you determine how to prove you are qualified if you are, and will help you become qualified if you still have some steps to take. I have attempted to go much further than to simply offer advice about how to better prove your competence. Developing and implementing strategies requires a constant awareness of context, so I have tried to make sense of the chaotic times in which we live and work. If we can't do this, if we cannot provide context, no amount of strategy development will help.

My intent is that this book will change forever the way you view the qualification process and that an enlightened perspective will keep you a step ahead of the game while helping to change the rules. I know how much anger and frustration credentialing problems can generate. My purpose in writing this book is to help you turn your anger into positive action. I recommend that you read this book over several times, pass it on to others and find the points upon which you agree and disagree. I further invite you to write us with your experience, your success stories, and your philosophical agreements and disagreements, both for our newsletter and as material for a companion volume to this book. Ongoing discussion and shared insight are vital to effecting change.

Chapter One

Changing the Focus to Outstanding Performance

If absolute power corrupts absolutely, academic power tends to corrupt absurdly.

—Charles J. Sikes

James R. Fisher Jr. says, "We are failing as a society because we are no longer organized to succeed."[1] Indeed, for decades, stratification within organizations has kept natural talent from advancing to where it is needed most. Rigid job descriptions cripple organizations in two fundamental ways. First, they use territorial boundaries to restrict tasks to specific individuals and groups. This is highly inefficient. Specific tasks have to be put off until someone "qualified" to perform them is found, even though the jobs are simple and can be performed by virtually anyone. The second effect is that these restrictions often prevent people with inborn talent from moving to higher levels within the organization. For example, clerical workers are restricted from management positions and laborers are forbidden to enter the technical sphere, even when they clearly demonstrate an aptitude for the work.

Matching talent to task is crucial to efficiency, effectiveness, and the management of quality. Rigid hierarchies based on occupational restrictions suffer a special kind of paralysis which inhibits creativity and discourages individuals from assuming responsibility. An ill-defined and uneasy alliance between business and educational institutions has created a caste system which, by nature of prior agreement, ensures its own predictions about success by allowing only those who pay their financial respects to educational institutions the opportunity to demonstrate their talents. The relationship of business and educational institutions is ill-defined because a direct connection with education and job performance is hard to shape. The uneasiness of the association rests upon this lack of a direct connection and the constant criticism businesses cast upon educational institutions for their failure to make the relationship perfect. Meanwhile educational institutions, both public and private, continue to promote passivity among students even though self-directed employees are what businesses really need.

The effective workplace is where theory and practice meet, making it imperative that on-the-job learning be both recognized and rewarded. The reason people in the workplace need to be self-directed is obvious: cutting-edge discovery is not a body of knowledge passed from one generation to the next. Discovery is a first-person enterprise. The very crux of meeting global competition head-on depends upon the efficiency of placing talent where it is needed, when it is needed, while assuring that those who use their talents are rewarded fairly. Instead of establishing sharp boundaries for job descriptions, we should be continually framing and reframing the question of how employees add value.² The bureaucratic nature of learning institutions ensures that, unless they are committed to cutting-edge research, they are likely to be far behind in the development of curricula. Worse still, as educator Page Smith observes in his book *Killing the Spirit,*

> The vast majority of the so-called research turned out in the modern university is essentially worthless. It does not result in any measurable benefit to anything or anybody. It does not push back those omnipresent "frontiers of knowledge" so confidently evoked; it does not *in the main* result in greater health or happiness among the general populace or any segment of it. It is busy work on a vast, almost incomprehensible scale.

Indeed, busy work and social status (not efficiency and effectiveness) have long dictated terms of employment. During times of strong economic growth, labor shortages cause less attention to be focused on qualifications and more directed toward finding people simply interested in working. Conversely, during economic downturns, educational inflation occurs: large numbers of unemployed college graduates cause employers to raise employment standards for everyone, regardless of whether or not there is a direct relationship between the nature of the qualifications and the work to be done. Reality suggests degrees have more to do with one's place in the employment line than with how one actually performs on the job. Thus, the cultural capital of education is simplified through the currency of credentials.

Merit and Achievement

Our expectations of merit—the way we go on and on about the importance of formal education—suggest we hold fundamental attitudes about the link between schooling and credentials and what it takes to become qualified for a particular job or position. But our actions—the way we treat our schools, pay our teachers, and support our students—suggest we don't really believe any of it. Moreover, by failing to *admit* what we really *know* or to acknowledge how we really feel about the fuzzy process of qualification, we set ourselves up for perpetual confusion and frustration.

In his book *What Color is Your Parachute?* (an annually updated, classic bestseller about job-hunting), Richard Nelson Bolles once referred to our method of seeking employment as a Neanderthal system. This description is too kind. The system we use, which is directly related to and a part of the whole process of "qualification," has more to do with denial and self-deception than with primitive notions. We have learned not to believe our first-hand observations about qualifications, while simultaneously relying on credentials based on qualifications. Our faith in and dependence upon authority cloud our thinking. We are further confused by our expectations in the workplace, because, as Bolles points out, people are often hired, promoted, and fired for reasons that have nothing whatsoever to do with qualifications. The person who observes such actions, without understanding the true reasons behind them, could easily draw erroneous conclusions about how to become qualified and could waste time running in circles as a consequence. By not thoroughly examining the process of qualification, a matter of central and pivotal importance in our lives, we have little choice but to deny our own experience.

Genuine experts (those with a lot of expertise) are painfully aware of their own ignorance and do not mind being asked questions beyond their ability to answer. But many who call themselves experts are insecure people who feign expertise and pretend to know far more than they do. This pretentiousness perpetuates a feeling among the general public that there is always someone with an answer for every question and that one can never be too sure of one's own knowledge, because there is sure to be an expert who knows more. Thus, we learn to doubt what we actually observe.

In the domain of work, we fail to acknowledge the individual who does a wonderful job but is without a credential (after all, one never knows what else the person lacks), and most of us support a system which will replace that person just as soon as someone with the proper credentials can be found. In a similar vein, we often deny the reality of the individual who seems to be well qualified, but who demonstrates such incompetence that everyone in the organization is distressed by it. In other words, in private, we really do know who performs well and who performs poorly, but in public—in plain view of those in charge of the organization—we admit nothing. We say nothing because we know the cost of admitting in public what everyone except upper management knows in private. Some are qualified, some are not, and that's the end of it. Philip Slater writes, "It is always tempting to attribute wisdom to people who claim it—especially when they have banded together and agreed to attribute it to each other."[3] Thus, our own opinions for evaluating standards of competence are null and void. I have known of managers who would use every type of rationale under the sun to defend people who were well "credentialed" but hopelessly incompetent—trouble at home, bad luck, a simple misunderstanding—even when the evidence of incompetence was overwhelming. And I have watched these same managers fail to promote individuals whose outstanding performance was just as self-evident because, in the manager's view, they were "not qualified."

During my early years in the workplace I used to think that these issues were simply matters of management prerogative. But, today, I believe that changing this irrational behavior is a moral and ethical imperative. Moreover, allowing others the authority to plan and control one's life is the same as abdicating responsibility for it. This issue is at the crux of our ability to compete globally, to achieve quality, to work safely, and to place work in peak harmony with sound mental and environmental health. We desperately need to bring the right mixture of knowledge, aptitude and experience to the jobs where these qualities matter most. And knowledge, no matter how it is acquired, should be recognized and honored. In his book *Deschooling Society*, Ivan Illich put this problem in perspective:

> Once we have learned to need school, all our activities tend to take the shape of client relationships to other specialized institutions. Once the self-taught man or woman has been discredited, all nonprofessional activity is rendered suspect. In school we are taught that valuable learning is the result of attendance; that the value can be measured and documented by grades and certificates.

In fact, learning is the human activity which least needs manipulation by others. Most learning is not the result of instruction. It is rather the result of unhampered participation in a meaningful setting. Our current educational system fails to acknowledge any learning settings except those provided by institutions. Our efforts to restrict the teaching of school to only those with ever-increasing credentials has produced one of the most ridiculed school systems in the developed world. We have a legion of "qualified" teachers in a school system that is "certified" as mediocre or worse. Why is freedom such an important aspect in every avenue of our lives except the freedom to learn? Illich continues,

> Insisting on the certification of teachers is another way of keeping skills scarce. If nurses were encouraged to train nurses, and if nurses were employed on the basis of their proven skill at giving injections, filling out charts, and giving medicine, there would soon be no lack of trained nurses. Certification now tends to abridge the freedom of education by converting the civil right to share one's knowledge into the privilege of academic freedom, now conferred only on the employees of a school. To guarantee access to an effective exchange of skills, we need legislation which generalizes academic freedom. The right to teach any skill should come under the protection of freedom of speech. Once restrictions on teaching are removed, they will quickly be removed from learning as well.[4]

Changing the current system means doing it one job at a time. To have any effect one must understand the nature of hierarchical power. Henry Kissinger once defined an expert as someone who can articulate the consensus of those in power. Imagine visiting an art gallery where all of the works of art are unsigned instead of a museum full of works by famous artists. Do you see the profound influence of cultural expectation? We're much more likely to see brilliance in art when society says it's there. Add a political definition to the term expertise and you can easily fathom the depths and grasp the magnitude of the power of hierarchies: people in charge must be knowledgeable because they are in charge. Might makes right.

Now, the proposed aim of a meritocracy is to reward achievement. On the surface it appears to be a noble idea. Indeed, I have no argument with the intention of rewarding effort. But we humans are self-protective creatures. We have a natural predisposition to view ourselves and those like us in a much better light than those from whom we feel distanced, those who are in some way different. We are literally geniuses at self-justification.[5] It's part of our makeup for survival. So, if we're not careful—very careful—we have a tendency to mistake *opportunity* for *achievement*. It is commonly believed that people who are financially able to go to better schools are naturally better achievers. After all, their grade point average proves this, doesn't it? Not true. All we prove by franchising opportunity is that "cultural capital" is transferable. In other words, people who have an advantage can pass it on. The history of educational achievement in America has recorded volumes of names of working class people whose support has enabled their children to graduate from college and enter a profession. This fact does not counter my argument about passing cultural capital on— it reinforces it. The first mistake we make is to automatically accept the myth that education necessarily improves people. The second is to assume that, when people with an advantage exert effort (as do those who go to college in order to graduate), their worth is exponentially magnified over those who did not advance the effort for lack of opportunity. This is a common but baffling phenomenon. It's like giving one child in a group a new bicycle and counting the child's effort to ride the bicycle up a hill as proof that this particular child should have been the one to receive the bicycle in the first place. Sadly, we are not engaged in a Darwinian struggle in which only those worthy of making a good living are the ones who get to and through school. Our political system has overwhelmed any such natural evolution. The major but subtle objective of our current educational system is to mirror the stratification of society in ways that those who provide financial support deem appropriate. If you don't believe this, stop conferring advantage on the sons and daughters of institutional benefactors and watch how quickly the contributions dry up.[6]

Our educational system is highly efficient at seeing that fortunate people are more highly valued than those who are unfortunate. Don't misunderstand my point, I'm not suggesting that we do not have exceptionally good institutions of higher learning in America. It's not the quality of the institutions, but rather the obstacles to access that I wish to hold to critical scrutiny, along with the erroneous assumption that a direct relationship exists between a college education and workplace performance. Most of the really large businesses and family fortunes existing in this country were created by people without college educations. Today most of those entrepreneurs would not even be allowed to fill out an application to work for the companies they themselves founded. That's not progress. What it is, is political power. The wrong kind of political power!

During the early days of the Prudhoe Bay oil field development on Alaska's North Slope, the excitement of a frontier undertaking was everywhere. Constructing a technically modern oil field in a hostile arctic environment was a challenge of the first order. These were high-paying jobs, and, as the field was brought on line, working conditions were always changing. People with extensive experience took the helm in a wide range of disciplines, and their performance was outstanding. They received merit pay and promotions. Their performance reviews read like heroic citations in a military campaign. And then, like a gigantic game of musical chairs, the music stopped. The frontier was tamed, the start-up excitement was over. Management changed, and so did its perception of expertise. Suddenly scores of people with demonstrated competence and outstanding performance histories were found to be "unqualified" for their positions. They were made to feel as if they were somehow counterfeit employees. Corporate managers from the home offices were horrified to discover many of those workers were lacking college degrees. Replacements with suitable credentials were soon found. Performance didn't improve, but corporate distress was alleviated.

Please don't misunderstand. I'm not implying a college education isn't good in and of itself. Instead, I'm trying to show the absurdity of perpetuating a stratified society based upon what really amounts to financial advantage and arbitrary requirements for advancement. Our massive credentialing system has not produced a cornucopia of risk-free professional services. Instead, when we examine the professions we find a small cadre of people who bring cutting-edge quality and distinction to their work, offset by a much larger group whose smoldering mediocrity and runaway malpractice have made us the most litigious society in the world.

Professionalism: Knowledge as a Franchise

The authors of *Power in the Highest Degree*, Charles Derber, William A. Schwartz, and Yale Magrass, have observed the following:

> In the class struggle over knowledge, the most essentially human gift, the right to enjoy creative thought and put one's ideas to work, becomes problematic for the mass of uncredentialed workers. Modern professionals, seeking to lock up knowledge as their private property, can set themselves against the most elementary creative needs of the rest of the population.

Credentialing tends to devalue inquiry. Evidence of credentials renders us less critical than we should be. In a variety of circumstances I have heard the remark, "Who is that person to be saying that?" Such a question reveals a lot about our society. The implication is that the right "who" can make any statement at all without having to justify its veracity. By focusing so strongly on credentials, we pay too much attention to the people who give advice and far too little to the advice itself.

Credentials act as barriers to thinking, when experience should warn us otherwise. A short history of the authority of knowledge would read: true today, false tomorrow. The earth is flat, then round. The sun revolves around the earth; no, the reverse. The very nature of what we call knowledge is fragile and precarious. Psychologists spend whole careers practicing brands of psychology based upon profoundly different models of human behavior: Freud, Adler, Skinner, Jung, Maslow, Rogers—take your pick. Whose theory of motivation is most accurate? Again, the authors of *Power in the Highest Degree* reflect:

> To this day, nobody has ever confirmed that most clients are actually cured or even helped by psychoanalysis. In a presidential address to the American Psychological Association, Carl Rogers presented evidence that practioners trained in graduate clinical psychology programs may be less effective than lay people acting as supportive friends. Yet analysts prosper.

The same problem exists in the field of nutrition. Today's health food is tomorrow's carcinogen. First sugar is good for you, then it isn't. Some thought sugar caused hyperactivity in children, but now they say it may have nothing to do with the behavior of children. Choose your food group, what was once a panacea is now at the root of disease. Again, this is not to say the effort of inquiry is unnecessary. Rather, it calls attention to a situation where people are afforded the franchise of expert status in occupations which, in time, turn out to be based on totally false assumptions. And, if that were not bad enough, the process of qualification itself makes orthodoxy more important than inquiry. In a system where qualification is so important, and so full of discrepancies, one would think there would be more people pointing out the inconsistency, but few are willing to risk questioning the status quo.

As strange as it may seem, many of the questions we pose about quality of work and quality of life would be answered readily, if we were to decredential our society and focus on outcomes more than on diplomas and certificates. This is a very simple, provable premise. But it is not so easy when we take a modern subject like psychology and say that humans are driven by the will, no the will to power, no the sex drive, no by simple behavioral reinforcement, no wait, it is by higher values that humans are driven. Wrong again, say the cognitive psychologists. It is by cognitive development, it is through psychobiology that we understand the motivations of human beings. Theories abound, and yet nothing seems clearly settled. Still a person can become an "expert," claiming any one of these views as being superior. Study almost any discipline, and you'll find that what was believed a generation ago is no longer considered to be true. Thus, many who have been afforded a franchised "lock" on knowledge in the past, have in fact been no closer to the truth than those who professed to know very little.

Of course, we have always considered an effort to learn and to "know" to be a noble undertaking, and I am not suggesting we stop doing so. But, surely, we have learned enough to know that human equality—which becomes equity in a society based on economics—is more important than what poses as temporary truth. If there is no effort to find truth, we are doomed to ignorance. But, if we franchise truth, we remain locked in ignorance for longer and longer periods, because we listen only to those who have a legitimate title to the truth and a deed to a highly paid job.

With regard to actual economic value, the only major difference between the professional and the blue-collar worker is the amount of money they are paid. Why do we pay much more to people whose lock on truth is so fleeting? The simple textbook answer is that we are trying to push the envelope of inquiry and gain new knowledge. Credentialism, though, stifles exploration because, unless one's questions are approved by the profession, they threaten it. Indeed, when knowledge is franchised by credentialism, not only do we learn to deny the validity of our own experience, we are also taught to depend upon "experts" because we can never trust our own judgment. And, although these "experts" often attempt to endear themselves to mere "lay-people," they nonetheless plant seeds of doubt about proceeding independently without their guidance. In his book *Information Anxiety*, Richard Saul Wurman writes,

> There is a tendency to believe that the more "expert opinions" we get—be they legal, medical, automotive, or otherwise—the more informed we will be. But we tend to forget that "expert opinion" is by no means synonymous with "objective opinion." Unfortunately, most experts come with a professional bias that makes obtaining truly objective information almost impossible. Take the second-opinion movement in medicine that is even being promoted by health-insurance programs, where patients are encouraged to consult more than one doctor before undergoing nonemergency surgery. Surgeons are trained to respond to problems by performing surgery, so it is likely that they will see surgery as the solution to a patient's problem.

Credentials are supposed to protect the public from unnecessary risk at the hands of those who provide us with a vast array of services, from teachers to physicians. But we know from practical experience that credentials in and of themselves are not sufficient proof of competence. Some high school graduates can't read. Many teachers, doctors and attorneys are highly credentialed but are, without a doubt, incompetent. My point is not to advocate elimination of credentials altogether, but to make achieving competence *more important* than the process of obtaining credentials.

Performance-based testing by institutions makes more sense than multiple-choice exams far removed from actual practice of the discipline being tested. Moreover, there is often no relationship whatsoever between classroom activities and the knowledge and skills required to actually perform jobs. "There has been little study of what is actually learned in school and how long it is retained. What evidence is available, though, suggests that schools are very inefficient places of learning."[7] So, it is not surprising that the workplace is a source of constant frustration and bewilderment for people who *can* perform well, but, lacking certain paper credentials, are passed over for promotion in favor of those who hide mediocre performance behind their degrees.

No, I don't maintain that colleges and universities should exist primarily for the sake of preparing people for the workplace. On the contrary, most work tasks do not approximate classroom activities. Have you ever performed any work that resembled the skills required for taking a multiple-choice test? So why is the ability to pass such tests taken as a prerequisite for tasks that require critical reasoning skills? Business leaders continually complain about the fact that students do not bring appropriate skills to the workplace, never realizing that, aside from questions of general literacy (which is a big problem), job-specific instruction is not the mission of higher education. We know that classroom experience is fundamentally different from on-the-job-experience. The more sophisticated work becomes, the less likely that schools will be able to provide a cutting-edge advantage.

The competitive economic structure of our system of higher education makes it necessary for those who administer it to act as if education were a scarce resource in order that people might be paid for imparting knowledge. In other words, we franchise what we think must be known so that teachers will be paid to teach. As a result, education becomes a business. It becomes desirable not to empower students quickly, but to keep them involved for longer and longer periods of time, thus bringing more money into the business. Again, I am not implying that we do not need institutions of higher learning. Rather, we need to restructure them so that it is in their economic interest to empower students quickly and that learning, regardless of its source, is recognized. In *The Credential Society*, Randall Collins writes:

> There is some tendency for technological advance to be associated with higher educational requirements, especially for blue-collar jobs. But the bulk of the evidence is in the other direction. Education is not associated with employee productivity on the individual level, and job skills are learned mainly through opportunities to practice them, as retraining proce-

dures for organizational innovations abundantly demonstrate. Social mobility surveys and observational studies of work both show that pressures for technical efficiency are submerged within the social struggles over positions, struggles in which membership in a cultural group is the crucial weapon.

It is not surprising, then, that educational credentials are most heavily emphasized within organizations stressing normative control—that is, cultural socialization...nor is it surprising that these are stronger determinants than technological change.

What schools could do, if we were to redirect their emphasis, is to teach students how to find multiple solutions to problems, how to think critically, creatively, and how to continually formulate better questions. This approach to learning would be as useful in individual lives as it would be in the workplace.

The current attempt to qualify people for jobs has become so great and so acute that educational institutions act as a monolithic personnel department for the United States, Inc. Students are screened for employment by grade point average. A genuine thirst for knowledge is not acknowledged as being important, nor are we equipped to discern who has it. In time, a student's short-term memory abilities will earn an approval slip which will be regarded as a passport and license for economic privilege. But the strength of Personnel USA does not depend upon the performance of its graduates nearly so much as on its ability to pronounce unworthy all of those who fail to pay their tuition. The path for competent people who have gained their knowledge in some way other than through a licensing institution can be permanently blocked. Many legal secretaries become better than the attorneys they work for at providing legal assistance to the general public in a multitude of circumstances ranging from the preparation of wills to simple divorce decrees, but they are never allowed to set up such a practice on their own. The result is that we pay outrageous prices for simple legal documents. Since teaching is a franchised business, freedom in learning is forbidden. Those who develop expertise on their own, in order to become certified, are apt to have to pay a partial tuition to an institution so as to honor its franchise on learning. This often involves fulfilling some arbitrary requirements made up by someone without any practical experience in that field.

The effects of this are far more serious and injurious to society than we realize. People become qualified for positions for which they are not suited, but they can't change to another occupation without great difficulty or bearing the expense of becoming qualified again. Those who are already franchised into a position of high income, as in the case of incompetent doctors, continue to "practice," and the public suffers the burden of injury. Critics of professionalism suggest that engineers are paid less well than doctors, not because their knowledge or skill is less, but because the results of their work are easier to judge.[8]

A system which values qualification more than actual competence accepts incompetence as a fundamental part of its basic structure. Professionalism does more to restrict opportunity than it does to produce quality or to protect consumers. Ironically, the most powerful message in our present system of qualification is that, by participating, one is paying one's dues, thus reserving one's place in line ahead of those with fewer opportunities. This ethos runs so deep that even people who despise and criticize the system, but who subsequently pay their own dues (by fulfilling formal educational requirements), become supportive of the system thereafter. "I had to go through the motions to qualify," they wail, "so everyone else should too." Never mind that the qualifying requirements were unnecessarily expensive, arbitrary, and superficial.

In a nutshell, my message is this: While proof of qualification is clearly necessary in the professions, the current system allows credentials to represent a transfer of power rather than demonstrated competence. The process often leads to pointless restrictions that prevent many talented people from realizing their full potential. You can have a good education without having credentials just as you can have credentials without a good education. There is almost a mystic aura surrounding the credentialed individual who is genuinely competent, but there should be none at all. After a time, people are either competent or they are not. Moreover, people practicing a profession to which they are not suited should not have to spend a lifetime trying to hide their lack of competence because it is too hard to change fields and begin the whole credentialing process over again. For the sake of quality and human dignity we need to rethink the entire process of education and its connection to workplace qualifications.

The computer has not only brought us myriad new product options, it has also cut to the quick of ambiguity about who really knows what they are doing and who doesn't. Software developers leave no room for doublespeak, sophistry, and ethereal snow-jobs about qualification. The results of their efforts are self-evident. Nobody cares how or where they learned their skill. In *High-Tech Jobs for Lo-Tech People*, William A. Schaffer writes about his experience in the high-tech field: "After almost twelve years working in it, I've become absolutely convinced that the high-tech industry is the most democratic there is. Once you are inside the walls, no one gives a damn about your degrees or your background." In his book

Profscam: Professors and the Demise of Higher Education, Charles J. Sikes makes a compelling case that the longer we tolerate the current practices in higher education, the more poorly we are served by them. Sikes demonstrates that professors spend less and less time teaching and more and more time depending upon low-paid teaching assistants to handle the actual job of instruction. Sikes argues that the quality of higher education increasingly suffers from larger and larger class sizes, subjects cloaked in stupefying jargon, and professors who are grossly under worked and overpaid. Many teach less than eight hours a week and pursue private entrepreneurial interests which have nothing, whatsoever, to do with teaching. Sikes describes it thus:

> A modern university is distinguished by costs that are zooming out of control; curriculums that look like they were designed by a game show host; nonexistent advising programs; lectures of droning, mind-numbing dullness often to 1,000 or more semi-anonymous undergraduates herded into dilapidated, ill-lighted lecture halls; teaching assistants who can't speak understandable English; and the product of this all, a generation of expensively credentialed college graduates who might not be able to locate England on a map.[9]

I would argue that the students who successfully navigate the domain of higher education and manage to learn something in the process do so because they take charge of their education themselves. Those who attend simply to become qualified have their ignorance certified, allowing them to demonstrate it subsequently as arrogance. Unfortunately, many people are surprised to discover that to "get an education" means one must ultimately take responsibility for one's own learning, whether it occurs in college or at the local library. Worse, those who do not attend college regard degree acquisition with a sense of awe that it does not deserve. There is nothing you cannot find out and learn on your own, if your desire to know is strong enough. Nothing.

Once again, the authors of *Power in the Highest Degree:*

> Experts can rarely *prove* the validity of their knowledge. Thus they must create a general perception of credibility, much as corporations do. The airlines reassure the public with images of rock-solid pilots in full-dress uniform. Pictures of shiny buses and cheerful drivers illustrate Greyhound's message that riders can relax and "leave the driving to us." Likewise, witch doctors often wore imposing headdresses. The medieval priest's robes, collars, crucifixes, even chastity vows, were symbols of virtue. Doctors, lawyers, and scientists today have their white coats, three-piece suits, certificates on the wall, and increasingly sophisticated advertising.

What we must do to fight the growing tendency to discredit the self-taught individual is to strip away the awe and mystique of these deceptive claims to economic franchise. If the witch doctor is to give us advice we must ask for removal of the headdress and demand unpretentious answers to our questions.

Decredentialing Society

Sociologist Randall Collins cites two healthy reasons for decredentialing society: "It would improve the level of culture within those schools that continue to exist, and it would provide the opening wedge of a serious effort to overcome inequality." [10] Even those of us in favor of abolishing our current system of credentialing must struggle to imagine being without it. Having been exposed to nothing else, we'd have difficulty letting it go all at once. But what we must realize is that formal schooling didn't become important until the mid-nineteenth century, even for the "professions," which at the time relied exclusively on the system of apprenticeship.[11] In his book *The Credential Society*, Collins describes how a decredentialed society might operate within the field of medicine:

> As it stands, American medical training is attached at the very end of a very long and expensive education that keeps the supply of physicians low and their incomes and social backgrounds very high. This formal education appears to have little real practical relevance; most actual training is done on the job in the most informal circumstances, through the few years of internship and residency. The existing medical structure is not only highly expensive, inefficient, and inegalitarian in terms of career access; but it is also tied to a system of job segregation in which the menial tasks are shunted off into a separate medical hierarchy of women with the assistance of low-paid ethnic minorities in service jobs with no career possibilities.
>
> It is likely that far greater quality and efficiency could be attained by eliminating the distinction between nurses and doctors and combining their career sequences with that of hospital orderlies. (No doubt this would offend the status concerns of doctors, but it would at least challenge them to take their altruistic claims seriously.) All medical careers would begin with a position as orderly, which would be transformed into the first stage of a possible apprenticeship for physicians. After a given number of years, successful candidates could leave for a few years of medical school (2 years seems sufficient background for most practitioners, and this could be done equally well at an undergraduate or postgraduate level, with the option being left open) and then return to the hospital for advanced apprenticeship training of the sort now given in internship and residency programs. The motivation of orderlies would be en-

hanced, and the implicit opportunities for apprenticeship-type training could simply be brought into the foreground. Advanced specialties could continue to be taught as they now are—through further on-job training; only medical researchers would be involved in lengthy schooling. The overall effect would certainly be less expensive and would provide better medical care from all personnel; there is no evidence to make one believe that the technical quality of treatment would suffer.

Imagine what a dramatic effect such a practice would have on the morale and motivation of a hospital staff, and on the patients' regard for the personnel. Respect for doctors would be based on the knowledge that they had a thorough understanding of the human condition from bedpan to scalpel. The mystique of medicine would diminish, but a genuine respect for the people who serve and are served by medicine would likely increase.

Once we take on a system as sacrosanct as the medical profession, the remaining professions seem relatively easy to decredential. Decredentialing society in the manner that Collins suggests would bring us closer to five objectives:

1. Better protection from incompetent practitioners.
   A. Classroom theory would be better balanced with hands-on experience.
   B. Actual performance would fall under the scrutiny of many associates, providing significant feedback for the quality of one's performance.
   C. The immediate opportunity for practical experience would allow people to judge in the early stages of training whether or not they were suited to such work, instead of spending years in a classroom for naught.
2. Superior economic equality.
   A. The time required for, and therefore the cost of, formal education would be greatly reduced. Economic, ethnic and gender barriers would thus be diminished.
   B. The costs of career preparation would be much less because training positions would be paying positions. In other words, one could *earn* one's way into a profession.
   C. In a system where everyone participates equally, where everyone understands the problems and concerns at each level of training, a more equitable pay structure would obtain. Even if a substantial number of people elected to remain at the middle or lower levels of a profession, the chances for an equitable salary would be enhanced.
3. Increased quality of service.

A. The environmental conditions for teamwork would be dramatically improved.

B. There would be no reason to hoard knowledge at any level.

C. The public would view working people with much more respect, leading to greater self-esteem among those workers. For example, any hospital orderly or staff law clerk would be viewed as a potential doctor or lawyer.

D. Apprenticed work would receive greater supervision than present systems allow—especially in medicine.

4. A greatly enhanced role for colleges and universities.

A. Without the need to act as employment screening agencies, colleges and universities could focus on promoting the intrinsic value of education.

B. Learning institutions could change from grade-driven curricula to student-centered, knowledge-centered agendas. If they failed to provide students with valuable knowledge, they would cease to exist.

C. With student-centered curricula, colleges and universities could compete to provide students with meaningful learning—they could achieve what Abraham Maslow called the ideal college which would be a place of essential self-discovery. Once such value existed, society would understand the need for these institutions, not just for our early years, but throughout our whole lives.

5. A superior society.

A. The redistribution of opportunity would lead to greater equality.

B. Having fewer people trapped in jobs they hate would significantly reduce our multibillion dollar stress industry.

C. The cost of goods and services would drop as the inflated cost of education decreased.

D. Finding one's right livelihood would be much easier. Having more people using their strengths in the right place would reduce frustration and increase efficiency and effectiveness.

The only way to make a good case for maintaining our credentialing system as it is today is to continue to deny the reality of our own experience. Those with a vested interest in the current system have the advantage of a monolithic bureaucracy which appears to be invincible, resisting all efforts to change it. Still, there may never have been a better time to battle the expansion of credentialism than the present. Consider the following statement by Alvin Toffler in 1970:

> Long before the year 2000, the entire antiquated structure of degrees, majors and credits will be a shambles. No two students will move along exactly the same educational track. For the students now pressuring higher education to destandardize, to move toward super-industrial diversity, will win their battle.[12]

Toffler's words might seem naive if we consider the apparent increase in demand for college degrees since 1970. But there is still time for his observation to prevail, and the need for it is growing exponentially. Nineteen years after Toffler's prediction, Peter Drucker wrote:

> For people without college credentials, business employment as worker or clerk is still the best available job opportunity. And for the foreseeable future, business will remain the largest employer of the poorly schooled. But these business jobs no longer represent the opportunity they did a hundred years ago; they have become dead ends.[13]

How can Toffler and Drucker both be right? Drucker goes on to speculate that during the next two decades the levels of management in American organizations will be significantly reduced.[14] His prediction says,

> A society dominated by knowledge workers makes even newer—and even more stringent—demands for social performance and social responsibility. Once again we will have to think through what an educated person is. At the same time, how we learn and how we teach are changing drastically and fast—the result, in part, of new theoretical understanding of the learning process, in part of new technology. Finally, many of the traditional disciplines of the schools are becoming sterile, if not obsolescent. We thus also face changes in *what* we learn and teach and, indeed, in what we mean by knowledge.[15]

Drucker argues that the emphasis is changing "from teaching to learning" and that "learning is as personal as fingerprints; no two people learn exactly alike." Precisely my point: as learning is acknowledged to be the province of individuality, the freedom to learn must follow. When you look deeply into these forecasts, it is apparent that Toffler and Drucker are making similar predictions, as you'll see in the following chapter.

Drucker made a further argument in 1993, that every service worker must have access to knowledge work. In *Post-Capitalist Society*, he writes,

The post-capitalist society has to create an educational system which, to use a computer term, offers "random access." Individuals must be able at any stage in their lives to continue their formal education and to qualify for knowledge work. Society needs to be willing to accept people into whatever work they are qualified for, regardless of their age.

No society is organized for this. In fact, most developed countries are organized to keep people in the station in which they begin their working careers. The system is most rigid in Japan, but nearly as rigid in Europe as well. The United States has gone furthest in creating educational opportunities for adults. The growth area in American education these last twenty years has been the continuing education of adults at any age, and the willingness to offer additional, more advanced knowledge in their specialties to already highly educated people. This gives the United States a tremendous advantage over other developed countries. But even in the United States, there is still reluctance to accept people in knowledge work unless they have acquired the basic qualifications fairly early in life.

Indeed, Robert M. Pirsig argues that "random access and quality are closely related."[16] Random access is an exquisite model for the idea of freedom because it emulates the activity of the human mind, the very basis of learning.

It is important to understand that the advantage the United States has in adult education has not been brought about by the propensity of colleges and universities to democratize education, but is instead driven by economics and demographics. American business has a colossal opportunity to once again move ahead of its competition by celebrating the freedom to learn. "Credentialism, while not legally binding, makes employers co-conspirators in the professional monopoly."[17] Business has the power over learning institutions because it uses them to screen employees. Parents and students would not pay outlandish fees to colleges if business did not honor the schools' franchise on learning. If business changes its hiring policies, colleges and universities will have no choice but to change as well. And, as paradoxical as it seems, business can save the technical side of higher learning by breaking the schools' choke hold on knowledge and opportunity. If educational institutions could be depended upon to send people into the workplace who are literate and able to take responsibility for their own learning, then business should reasonably expect to bear the costs of education particular to each industry. It makes far more sense for employees to earn their way into occupations than to go deeply into debt on the hope of landing a good job.

Dynamic learning requires that learning institutions be "open systems."[18] But to break a system open, we must thoroughly understand why it is closed. Chapter Two will point out the cracks in the structure and help us get a foot in the door.

Chapter Two

Understanding What You Are Up Against

The Achilles' heel of authoritarianism is that the leader by the very nature of his position is able to ignore the wisdom of anyone "below" him—that is, anyone who stands between him and the real world. This is what authority means: immunity from competence.

—Philip Slater

The Dynamics of Pyramid Power

A few decades ago, before the new age era, an unusual fad hit with a great deal of fanfare. It was called pyramid power. Proponents (there are probably still a few around) claimed that the fundamental architecture of the pyramid caused a vast assortment of paranormal phenomena, including the power to heal the body and to sharpen dull tools. Belief in pyramid power quickly faded, but I have never been able to forget it. As I see it, we are subject to pyramid power on a far greater scale than ever imagined by those who hoped to sharpen razor blades. It is ubiquitous, and it affects us deeply: I am talking about the power of hierarchy.

This phenomenon is easy to observe in lower primates but it is difficult to understand within our own society, especially in institutions. The principle of the power of hierarchy provides the structure for all of our organizations, even the one we call the family. Organizations are driven by personality and the friction of hierarchical relationships. Here, merit and achievement, by design, are totally dependent upon the power of hierarchy. Failure to understand the psychology of hierarchies will ensure a life of bewilderment. The world of status, rank, bosses and subordinates is confusing, not because it's complicated, but because it has always been with us. We take it so much for granted that we never think to question it.

Organizations bring forth tribal tendencies in human beings. They offer differing forms of security and advantage in exchange for some type of effort, commitment, or loyalty. The security gained resembles that found in families, which form the core of tribal societies. And it's instant. As soon as you join, you belong.

Organizations create their own culture: their own ways of doing things, their own totems and symbols of power. Potted plants in the corner and oil paintings on office walls give evidence of one's tribal standing. An associate of mine once made the mistake of spending some of her own money to decorate her office. She added a carpet, greenery, and a wall hanging. The room looked better than her boss's office—a taboo of the greatest magnitude. Her action caused an incredible stir which required the immediate remedy of putting everything back the way it was.

An organization's culture is the synergistic effect of its attitudes, habits, rules, regulations, written and unwritten policies. The older and larger the organization, the more likely its culture will be stronger, deeper and—like a river—harder to move against. One must never forget that the source of this river is drawn from a pool of pyramid power—power by association. A person's standing in a hierarchy—and not necessarily individual merit—is often all it takes to be privy to the kind of inside information that enables one to maintain such a standing in the first place. We've all heard the management principle which says "excrement" runs downhill. We know this means that trouble felt in the higher echelons of a hierarchy means trouble for those at the lower levels. But what is not so clear is how this form of power creates its own culture with far-reaching but little-recognized effects. To appreciate the full meaning of my claim you have only to remember Watergate, Chernobyl, Challenger, the Bay of Pigs, the Navy and Clayton Hartwig, the Tailhook convention, the Iran Contra affair and Col. North, the savings and loan crisis of the late '80s, or the Anita Hill-Clarence Thomas confrontation. In each of these instances the vividness of normally hidden power of the pyramid comes to the surface. We see the grain of the organization and the cost for cutting against it. Each time this type of incident occurs, most of us feign some degree of shock, which is the same as denying that we ourselves are subject to such power or that we are in any way influenced by these pervasive forces.

Watergate and Chernobyl illustrate the pains to which subordinates will go to protect their superiors. The Bay of Pigs incident demonstrates how the influence of the power of hierarchy is so authoritarian as to create an atmosphere of practical denial where everyone is afraid to tell the boss (in this case President John F. Kennedy) the truth.

Recall that during the Clarence Thomas-Anita Hill hearings, members of the U.S. Senate repeatedly expressed "outrage," not at the possibility of someone being appointed to the Supreme Court who didn't belong there, but because someone had the audacity to challenge *their* authority and "leak" accusations about a Supreme Court candidate. Never mind that they'd do the same without blinking, if the need arose. Those hearings revealed subtle aspects of the power of hierarchy that are seldom brought to light. For example, in almost every major city in the U.S. a candidate for police officer is required to take a polygraph examination, but to even suggest that a candidate for the U.S. Supreme Court take a polygraph examination (even when accused of degenerate behavior) was supposed to be insulting and laughably unnecessary. (Anita Hill, on the other hand, agreed to and passed a lie detector test). This is the residue of the power of hierarchy. In the course of a career a police officer will touch the lives of maybe a few thousand people. But a Supreme Court justice can affect millions over generations with a single decision.

In the nuclear power industry we have yet to create an organization that is free from the universal control of the dominance of hierarchy. Studies confirm that, throughout their history, almost all of our nuclear power plants have silently exposed their neighbors to excessive radiation (this is even worse in developing countries). Because of the power of hierarchy, though, it was almost impossible to make these facts public. In most cases, full disclosure was not made until years after the incidents occurred.

The power of hierarchy is the same phenomenon which has increasingly transferred the burden of taxes from corporations to individuals. Thus, even though productivity has increased steadily for generations, it now takes two incomes to support the average family instead of one. Power and authority are necessary so that organizations may have the capability of meeting their objectives, but power has a lot in common with radiation: the opportunity for overdose increases exponentially with its use. Once a mishap occurs with power, contamination is a problem of monumental consequence which can rarely be undone. Power, like radiation, does not give up life easily. It is shared through the process of self-preservation. In other words, acts on the part of individuals to protect their organizations from harm become the substance of social union which compels them to affirm authority at any cost.

During the space shuttle Challenger hearings in 1987, the iconoclastic physicist Richard Feynman placed a rubber O-ring component into ice water to demonstrate simply and clearly how the rubber could lose elasticity. Perhaps you, too, at that moment began to feel a sense of rage at the association of hierarchies who were trying to make a simple engineering problem so obscure that the general public could not comprehend it. Again, the real viciousness that can accompany the power of hierarchy is apparent when you examine an incident like that involving the U.S. Navy and Clayton Hartwig, where the Navy tried to ruin a deceased sailor's reputation rather than find fault with its own policies and procedures. The amount of effort a large bureaucratic organization will expend to protect its senior members (Tailhook is another example) is unconscionable. The Iran Contra (arms for hostages) affair showed how the ideology of patriotism can be perverted by hierarchy. Col. North claimed patriot status while his actions deprived the rest of us of our rights to representation.

Once you fully realize the potency of this covert but implicit force, the map of your own journey through life will be better marked. Land mines stand out and you begin to appreciate how easy it is to unintentionally call in a volley of artillery on your own coordinates. Once the dynamism of the power of hierarchy is visible, the actions and behavior of the participants within a hierarchy make more sense. The omnipotence of the power of hierarchy explains how executives can demand that pay be tied to performance and yet, when their own companies begin losing millions of dollars and must lay people off, they continue to draw obscenely enormous salaries and finally bail out with golden parachutes.

In *The Wish For Kings*, Lewis H. Lapham writes,

> By 1991 the average pay of the average company chairman exceeded the average pay of the average worker by a ratio of 93 to 1, but despite the conventional announcements about a man's worth being measured by his achievement, corporate executives get paid according to the weight of their acquaintance and the number of strata below them in the table of organization.

Hierarchically designed organizations have an undeserved association with efficiency. In his book *The New Achievers*, Perry Pascarella describes how hierarchical design contributes to systematic suppression in the workplace. He uses an example of getting a check approved at a department store:

> It seems that whenever the customer lines are longest at her cash register, someone presents a personal check. The clerk is not allowed to approve the check, however. She is looking at the customer. She can inspect his proof of identity. But company

rules say she must go to a supervisor who has the "authority" to approve acceptance of the check. That supervisor may be a sixteenth of a mile across the store, but she has the red pen with which to indicate official approval. Without seeing the customer or his identification, the supervisor places her initials on the check, thereby permitting business to resume.

Now, of course, when the clerk returns to her register, the line will be longer, the customers will be more impatient, but she will know who is in charge, who is expected to think and who is not, while the store will be no less apt to receive a bad check than before. Pyramid-type organizations are bureaucratic by design, the head is severed from the hands. Rules substitute for reason.

Whistle Blowers and Palace Guards

Hierarchies are intuitively savvy about blame and sacrifice. They are sort of Zen-like in that they redirect culpability to the lowest level of organizational influence. This doesn't even need to be taught; everyone just seems to know in advance who the best candidates are for the sacrificial alter. It's an assumption which acknowledges that occasionally someone has to pay for the sins of the organization.

There are two types of people in every large organization: those who *affirm* the power of the hierarchy and those who *threaten* it. Their actions range from those of palace guards to those of whistle blowers. The principle they share in common is that each individual carries these actions out either overtly or covertly. Col. North is an example of the latter. We know who the palace guards are when their actions are overt (we call them names I won't repeat here). We may suspect who they are when they ridicule the organization in the company of lower level workers but support the authority of the organization in private by spying for the bosses (we call them traitors). Similarly, we may suspect who the whistle blowers are when their actions are covert, but they are easy to identify when they act overtly because they become *the people who used to work here*.

The mysterious source of power in organizations rests upon twin pillars: one is political (power by and through association); the other comes from knowledge or expertise (which may be technical or theoretical). The source of power usually depended upon by palace guards is political in nature, while whistle blowers rely on critical discourse or technical expertise which challenges the wisdom of authority.

Understanding the power of hierarchy in this context is necessary to a person's well being in an organization, and it often has more to do with getting promoted than does one's level of competence. There are many examples of whistle blowers who have saved lives and millions of dollars by calling dangerous or inefficient practices into question, only to be fired later, even when their efforts were brought to the attention of the public through the media. Sometimes the power of hierarchy is influenced by public outrage and sometimes it is not. It can seem as forceful as gravity itself. A worker dies somewhere in America every few hours due to unsafe working conditions. But the power of hierarchy is so pervasive that our attention is deflected and we focus instead on the ridiculousness of OSHA regulations.

Levels of Organizational Reality

Another component critical to the understanding of the power of hierarchy is the varying levels of reality in organizations. These become clearer when placed in parallel with the management of a ship at sea. A typical ship has a captain, a staff of officers, and a crew, all of whom are highly dependent upon one another. Nevertheless, reality for the captain is quite different than it is for the crew. The captain is concerned with the ship's mission, its destination. The crew is concerned with a myriad of details that are critical to reaching the destination, yet have little to do with the subject of the destination. The crew can work for months without knowing where they are going. The officers have yet another reality. They, too, are concerned with the destination of the ship, and they may have extensive technical competence—some may actually set the course the ship follows. But the officers are far more concerned with what the captain thinks than with the mission itself. This same analogy can apply to the relationship between the officers and the crew. In other words, the crew members may at times be more concerned with what the officers think than with the details of their individual jobs.

I raise this issue to illuminate three levels of valid reality: one of vision, one of behavior, and one of technical knowledge. All three realities are important, misunderstood, underappreciated, and underutilized. If the captain lacks vision, the ship may sail in circles and finally run aground or worse. If the crew doesn't know what they are doing, anything might happen—the ship could blow up or sink. If the officers can't get along, there might be mutiny. Imagine the complexity of the struggle for power in an organization with 15 or more levels of management, as was once the case with American automobile manufacturers. This picture indicates how moving up through the ranks would involve adopting a new perspective, but it also calls attention to the extraordinary force of the power of hierarchy: regardless of your visionary or technical level of expertise, behavior will always count disproportionately more.

Never forget that affirming the organizational hierarchy has always been a priority of the first magnitude. The unemployment line is filled with people who fail to acknowledge this reality. I'm not for a minute suggesting that a person should always go along with authority for safety's sake. There are ways to deal effectively with problems when there is a conflict within an organizational hierarchy, but they require knowledge of the opposition. As in the martial arts, the basic principle is to deal with a direct force by redirecting it. Redirecting attention toward a problem greater than your current predicament while simultaneously offering myriad solutions is one example. The more layers of management, the taller the pyramid, the greater the capacity for downward political pressure. Ignorance in these matters will ensure nothing but tire tracks across your back.

The political power which exists within an organization is intensified, in part, by the fact that most modern organizations are built on an educational credential basis which would not occur in a primitive state of nature. For example, in a group of primates—say chimpanzees or gorillas—the group assumes a hierarchical order based upon self-evident strength and temperament. But, in a human organization, we most often assume a formal hierarchy based upon education and credentials. Sometimes education may represent real superiority, and sometimes it has no bearing, whatsoever—especially in situations where there is no direct relationship between the education represented by the credential and the actual work at hand. People who might have naturally been Alpha (dominant) males and females in a primitive society can be held to the roles of subordinates in today's organizations because of the arbitrary nature of credentials.

Hierarchies that depend too heavily upon educational credentials create organizations in which a significant number of people will feel—consciously or unconsciously—that the hierarchy is artificially contrived and is thus unjust. This phenomenon manifests when individuals become extremely sensitive to interactions with persons they feel have no business giving them work direction. If you've been in the workplace for a long while, you may be able to relate to this directly. How many times have you gritted your teeth in a subordinate role which you thought should be reversed? The contrast becomes even clearer when we willingly take direction from someone we admire, someone whom we think should hold superior rank.

Now, it is my theory that this resentment, based upon an inchoate sense of unfairness, gives strength to the power already available (by design) in a hierarchy. The power of any level in a hierarchy is actually enhanced if it is resented because the people who resent it will go to incredible efforts to avoid any appearance of being disciplined by people they don't respect. I have witnessed countless incidents where a person in a superior role makes a mild-spoken but slightly negative comment to a subordinate who thereafter attests to having been chewed out unmercifully. It is both ironic and unfortunate that the design of the hierarchical organization in and of itself contributes to its power in such a way that an ill-designed organization may have more power to command than one thought to be built upon sound merit. A dysfunctional organization may have more power by nature of coercion than a psychologically well-balanced organization does through cooperation. For many of us, it is an even worse abuse to have to endure praise from someone undeserving of the privilege of giving it. Though we seldom think of giving praise as an exercise of power, it is something everyone understands at a visceral level. Hence, as a general rule, subordinates do not go around saying "great job" to the boss.

Knowledge and Organizations

In his book *Earthwalk*, Philip Slater wrote,

Institutions are like trees. The green living part consists of relationships between people. As these become habitual they leave a dead deposit in the form of structures and procedures. Like a tree trunk, the dead deposit grows continually larger, while the living matter clings to the outside of it. The dead tissue of the trunk is much easier to understand than the living tissue of the bark, and can be more easily dealt with in qualitative terms. It is easy to lose sight of where the life is because the tree still looks very imposing after it is completely dead.

It is in the nature of the power of hierarchy to relegate people who appear to threaten its omnipotence to the dead part of the tree.

To be current and realistically up-to-speed in most dynamic or cutting-edge disciplines is to embrace confusion. Confusion is a natural state, a desirable state for those who expect to break through barriers of knowledge. Confusion spurs us to overcome it, to understand to such a degree that we'll push through to a new level of understanding and thus reach yet another state of confusion. But if this is not well understood organizationally (as is the case in most organizations not deeply concerned with research) the appearance of confusion will be organizationally unacceptable. After all, educated, credentialed people are supposed to have the truth nailed to the wall. And many times it is the pretense of having it hammered down that keeps us from finding it. In an organization where people feel it necessary to hide their lack of knowledge, one doesn't want to be seen asking questions.

In his book *The Fifth Discipline*, Peter M. Senge writes,

> School trains us never to admit that we do not know the answer, and most corporations reinforce that lesson by rewarding the people who excel in advocating their views, not inquiring into complex issues. (When was the last time someone was rewarded in your organization for raising difficult questions about the company's current policies rather than solving urgent problems?)

Senge describes a training exercise led by Donella Meadows in the late 1970s. Called "The Wall," it was designed to help people develop insight in comprehending the complexity of extensive problems. The workshop on Third World malnutrition was conducted in the presence of respected experts. As the chart used for developing an overview of the intricate relationships and feedback loops grew more and more complex, an experienced lobbyist begin to moan audibly while shaking her head. Asked if she the were ill the lobbyist replied, "My God. All my life, I assumed that somebody, somewhere, knew the answer to this problem. I thought politicians knew what had to be done, but refused to do it out of politics and greed. But now I realize that nobody knows the answer. Not us, not them, not anybody."[1]

I know exactly how she felt. For years, before I began my own enterprise of self-education, I thought that society's credentialed elites had the truth by the jugular in most important matters. But it has become clearer and clearer to me that such appearances are often more dependent upon the design of organizations than on reality.

For years it has been politically correct to say that no one knows more about a particular job than the person doing it. This philosophy doesn't fare so well in actual practice, as evidenced by the sheer number of decisions made about jobs without consulting those who are doing them. In tough, competitive economic times, however, it makes startling sense to assume the person doing the job knows more about it than anyone else. It is also cheaper and more efficient to ask their opinion often and to include them in planning for the future. A positive aspect of downsizing and global competitiveness is that it's becoming more and more practical to treat workers like adults. The dark side of this practice is that for many in lower level, service sector jobs the reverse is true. They will be treated more and more like children and will be treated with less respect than ever before.

Times Are Definitely Changing

For generations the rhetoric in American business perpetuated the illusion that we Americans were somehow innately superior to the citizens of other nations and that our successful business enterprises offered clear-cut proof of our superiority. When we were the world's only major manufacturer of automobiles, profits could bear any inefficiency. Layers upon layers of management could swell the bureaucracy, and consumers still had to pay the price if they really wanted to drive a car. Indeed, profit bore the additional cost of hiring people screened through educational institutions and lacking practical skills. But, today, the bare facts of global competition are eating away at our illusion.

The paradigm has changed. American management is paying a price for the lip service it used to give to excellence without taking action. It may be more correct to say that American workers are paying a high price for mismanagement. Indisputable competence is becoming important, really important, perhaps for the first time in the history of American business. And, if competence can be acquired by our global competitors without paying for educational inflation, (by hiring and training employees who have not had to finance an overly-expensive education) we will have to do likewise. Similarly, if our global competitors make use of relevant, esoteric education and special training, we must also follow suit. The new bottom line is going to demand that we recognize competence regardless of its educational source, the same way that we now recognize quality products regardless of who in this world makes them.

Fast times require accelerated learning strategies. People who can demonstrate that they can take charge of their own learning are beginning to stand out and will soon be in greater demand than ever before. Moreover, the days are numbered for antiquated curricula, with their decade-old textbooks, to remain acceptable as preparation for cutting-edge skills. It is a glaring example of the tumultuous times in which we live, that as more and more knowledge is gained in more and more disciplines, we are simultaneously witnessing the unraveling of the expert. The ability of any individual or group to lay claim to absolutes is severely impaired when myriad opinions to the contrary are instantly available via the Internet. Our increasing ability to scrutinize the assertions and opinions of experts shifts the responsibility for making informed decisions from the expert to the questioner—as it should.

Flattening the Pyramid

For many years we have been learning (mostly the hard way) that authoritarianism is not the paragon of efficiency we once thought it was. Real efficiency places knowledge where it is needed, when it is needed, without delay. Moreover, we are *beginning* to learn that strengthening employee relations is the most effective way of improving customer relations.

Management gurus all over the country have been talking for more than a decade now about the flattening of the organizational pyramid. The buzzword "empowerment" has steadily gained acceptance, though hundreds of thousands of workers now wince when they hear it as a result of having been "empowered" at one time or another. James R. Fisher says our current manic obsession with quality is experienced as "a *stylistic overlay*, superimposed on workers by management."[2] I believe we are moving toward a flattening of the organizational pyramid, but the road ahead will still be crooked and rough.

There are benefits to be gained from flattening the pyramid that are not so readily apparent: if there are fewer bosses, people are *more* likely to be held accountable for their performance because more people of equal rank will rely directly upon one another. Peter Drucker suggests that the word "rank" is likely to disappear from our work vocabulary,[3] and that "knowledge employees cannot, in effect, be supervised. Unless they know more than anybody else in the organization, they are to all intents and purposes useless."[4]

Downsizing

On a personal level, downsizing amounts to being fired. In an organizational sense it is called a laying off. Corporate "spinmasters" call it "rightsizing," or "streamlining" to suggest that it is a necessary move to become "lean and mean" and to better compete globally. The corporate downsizing now underway, and likely to continue for years, is in part a reluctant admission that the traditional hierarchy is inefficient. The illusionary bubble of our inherent superiority has burst. Political power—power by association—is becoming less reliable. Power based upon actual knowledge is becoming more and more important. The Japanese, the Germans, and others quietly stepped ahead in many areas of technology, while American management daydreamed about excellence for others. The percentage of the American work force classified as managers is more than three times that of the Japanese and more than double that of the Germans. It is little wonder that the foreign businesses are more efficient—they have more workers working.

Here at home, downsizing has contributed substantially to reducing layers of management. Peter Drucker has predicted that during the next two decades America's management ranks will be reduced by two-thirds.[5] And Fisher says that "one day soon, in the blinking of an eye, the organization will be transformed from authoritative control to egalitarian consensus."[6] I hope he's right, even though those of us who are middle-aged today will probably be retired before the pyramid has truly flattened in most organizations. The reason for this has much more to do with learned behavior than with intellectual resistance. Despite management's queasiness about genuine empowerment, the benefits of achieving it are easy to see. But it's not nearly as easy to change deeply ingrained behaviors that have a way of surfacing during times of high stress. People who have learned a vast repertoire of strategies for survival within a hierarchy will resort to them when the going gets tough, no matter what the corporate cheerleaders are saying. A former chief executive of IBM recently abandoned his usual positive predictions about the future and began blaming lower level employees for business losses while most industry analysts blamed upper management.

Managers who do not value the fundamental strengths of those who are different from themselves tend to use downsizing as a means for recreating the organization in their own image. They keep all of the employees who share their dominant strengths and dismiss the ones who don't. The inevitable result is that their strengths will now become weaknesses, because the balancing strengths are gone. When managers who truly believe in empowerment move on and are replaced by less enthusiastic supporters of the idea of sharing power, the old pyramid springs back to life.

In the short-term, downsizing increases the power of hierarchy because of what I call the *willingness factor*. This term describes a very simple premise: hard times spark a significant increase in what people are willing to do to survive economically. A willingness to carry out the will of the employer is greatly enhanced when one's job is on the line, often with minimal reflection given to the effects of one's actions. In a job seekers' market, the willingness factor moves the other way. But, when jobs are scarce people, take classes and special courses designed to help them say exactly what the employer wants to hear in a job interview, regardless of whether or not it is true.

It should not be surprising, then, that democracy itself is best assured when the willingness factor among the general population is fairly low and autocratic posturing is open to attack. Nor should it be lost on us that one of the greatest fears of those in the upper echelons of society is an erosion of their authority when people in the lower ranks become too comfortable and the willingness factor wanes. The consequences of poverty serve the powerful in any country by providing examples of what will happen to those unwilling to do their bidding, even though willingness may have little to do with the causes of poverty. A prolonged high-willingness factor gives rise to tyrants in both industry and government. Moreover, let history not forget that the greatest gains made by ordinary workers in this century were made when the willingness factor was at its highest during the depression of the 1930s.

Employee Leasing

The original purpose of employee leasing (at least the way most of us understood it) was to assist in the growth and development of small business and to extend benefit packages to the employees of small companies who would otherwise not be able to afford them. Employee leasing was to make small business flexible and efficient. But the end result of employee leasing has been that big corporations have been able to escape the traditional employee-employer contract and pay workers less in actual wages and benefits for performing identical jobs.

Nearly a decade ago, many managers in large corporations feared the judicial system would intervene and conclude that employee leasing was nothing more that what it is: a sophisticated effort to pay lower wages. Corporate leaders feared the consequences of appearing to have a two-tiered work force where two people performing the same task side by side would receive different rates of pay, one high (a traditional company employee) and one at a lower rate (a leased employee). Great precautions were taken to see that the leased employee took direction only from a leased supervisor so that their work tasks appeared temporary and contingent. Maintaining a distance between regular personnel and leased employees was supposed to enhance the temporary appearance of the arrangement, even though there was nothing at all interim about it.

Today, the ubiquity of employee leasing has all but alleviated any apprehension on the part of management about any action by the courts. For now, employee leasing has the appearance of being the wave of the future, even if it drowns a large segment of our population. It is not all bad as we shall see. A phenomenon, even less openly recognized is that a great many service businesses (fast-food franchises among them) actually implement strategies to encourage high employee turnover for the sole purpose of keeping wages low. For generations the ethos of the employment contract rested upon the notion that good help while hard to find was even harder to keep. It is hard—very hard—for many people to realize that this premise has radically changed: long-term employees in many low-level, service-type jobs expect increasingly higher wages in return for their loyalty. High turnover solves this problem.

There is a brighter side to temporary or contract employment. For many people it offers a flexible independence, an ability to travel, to sample occupations, to network and make new friends and contacts, to learn new systems, and to acquire universal skills. And, for some, contract employment results in higher wages and more employment benefits than they would have acquired otherwise in a more traditional employment role. For still others, contract employment leads to more permanent employment.

Times are definitely changing. Careers, more and more, are becoming series of related work experiences instead of single trajectories within one business. For those who must prove they're qualified, the good news is that downsizing, employee leasing, and the flattening of hierarchies have made genuine competence patently more important than it has ever been.

Chapter Three

Understanding Management

Only mediocrities rise to the top in a system that won't tolerate wavemaking.

—Laurence J. Peter

To appreciate the dynamics and frailties of management we must put the subject into historical perspective. Millions of us enter the work force each year believing that our work efforts will mirror those of generations of workers before us, but how we define work, and what we believe about those who do it, are constantly changing. Modern studies of primitive people and evidence left behind indicate that hunter-gather societies sustained themselves nicely on about four hours of what we would call work each day. Their artifacts suggest they found meaning and significance in almost everything they did. We, on the other hand, work from eight to twelve hours a day and consider the search for meaning to be a special business.

Since the Reformation, work has been considered a curse, an atonement for sin and evidence of moral virtue. Modern management has roots in some of the most horrendous practices of human relations imaginable, ranging from the forced labor and routine beating of children to manipulation of clocks and cheating workers out of time when only factories had clocks.

One of the underlying assumptions held by management has been that a major function of technology is to replace workers with machines. When he was a professor of economics at Harvard, Secretary of Labor Robert B. Reich wrote:

> No one can anticipate the precise skill that workers will need to succeed on the job when information processing, know-how, and creativity are the value added. Any job that could be fully prepared for in advance is, by definition, a job that could be exported to a low-wage country or programmed into robots and computers; a routine job is a job destined to disappear.[1]

Indeed, in this century, the concept of management has changed significantly, and a dramatic shift is now underway.

The Changing Face of Management

During the '40s and '50s we followed the management principles of "Classical Management" set forth by Frederick W. Taylor. Mistaken assumptions taken from Taylor's work suggested that workers must have their work planned by others because people are naturally lazy. The crux of Taylor's theory lay in the hypothesis that an autocratic work environment is efficient—an idea which seems logical on the surface but is, in fact, antithetical to democracy. Clearly, an autocratic management hierarchy can appear to be efficient in a manufacturing setting that is standardized and uncomplicated. But, in a highly technical workplace, where precision and quality are critical, the democratic ability to place authority for decision making at the same level where it is most often used is the most efficient and effective method of managing.

Since the 1940s American management has experimented with a multitude of theories, all aimed at maximizing productivity while maintaining control. In practice, this has played out like a game of tug-of-war on a continuum of centralized versus decentralized authority. Management lets the rope go for a while in the direction of decentralization, but it always pulls back, lest its own existence be threatened. Management fads have ranged from creating a happy work force, with the expectation that happy people work harder, to adopting the tidy formulas of *The One Minute Manager,* which results in a simplistic, paternalistic stance that, in my opinion, actually exacerbates the problems associated with hierarchies.

By its very nature management is a subjective enterprise. Managers exercise prerogative and personal opinion every time they review performance. In the name of objectivity they subjectively judge performance, producing a range of acceptability as a standard for each job reviewed. Of course, the size of this margin depends upon the nature of the work. When the consequences for error are extremely high, the margin may be very small. When the consequences are less apparent, the margin or standard for performance may allow a wider range of tolerance.

The hierarchical design of organizations encourages subjective confusion. Managers judging other managers who judge the performance of employees whose work takes place beyond their own observation is hazy and obscure at best. First, there is the fact that each of us is different, with different talents and personalities. Each of us, therefore, values performance differently. Now, compound this with the fact that there are two fundamental ways of approaching management: one focuses on "doing things right" while the other focuses on "doing the right things."[2] There is a profound difference between these two approaches. The first produces a seedbed for finding fault and yields a perennial harvest of blame. Personalities in this environment assume a defensive posture; creativity and innovation may be sacrificed for "playing it safe." On the other hand, "doing the right things" tends to focus on the system, enabling everyone to concentrate on the objective at hand instead of trying to stay out of trouble. If Thomas Edison had concentrated on "doing things right," most likely someone else would have invented the light bulb.

Quality, price, and product or service distribution may fluctuate wildly if there's too much focus on "doing things right," because there is little allowance for flexibility. Whereas "doing the right things" is a strategy which always takes variables into consideration. A key to success is to make use of both strategies: discovering the right things to do and then doing them right, without letting one of the practices exclude the need for the other. But this is a lot easier to say than to do. The need for good hamburgers hasn't changed over the years, but the very nature of restaurant fare has. "Fast food" has radically changed the concept of service and delivery. Those whose only focus was good food may still be in business, and they may even be prosperous, but those who concentrated on quality and consistency in food, service, and delivery became McDonald's, Burger King, and Wendy's.

Just as there are two fundamental ways of approaching management from a how-to perspective, there are also two fundamental types of knowledge: technical and nontechnical, sometimes characterized as *esoteric knowledge* versus *common sense*. When you consider management in light of these issues, it's easy to see what happens when those who manage do not have a good understanding and appreciation of both. MBA's who try to manage an organization, without appreciating the natural differences a large number of people contribute in terms of knowledge and skills bring to that organization, are likely to fail as managers. They may be able to produce an acceptable bottom line, if they are in the right industry, at the right time. But, in a highly competitive, volatile environment, they are often unequivocal failures. This is clearly evidenced in the performance of the automotive executive in pre-Japanese manufacturing days. The old manager may have been able to coerce and alienate the work force and still maintain market share, but, today, nothing less than the work force's total enthusiasm and personal commitment will do to match global competition. Failure to understand the broad range and natural distribution of strengths and weakness in our society tends to fool managers into thinking that the only valid perspective in viewing the workplace is their own. Such managers receive reinforcement for this view from their closest subordinates since, in all likelihood, those are the ones who share the values of the manager. To be sure, there are times when certain values are more appropriate to an organization than others, but the manager who does not understand the perpetual need for balance is like a deaf symphony conductor who does not realize it when many of the orchestra members aren't playing.

Managers rarely have sophisticated know-how in both technical and nontechnical areas. In other words, they are either highly technical, with limited knowledge of the people-side of management, or their strengths are reversed and their people skills are greater than their technical skills. This situation is the result of regarding school performance as the decisive factor in choosing who will get a particular job: we still wind up with nontechnical people in jobs where technical skills are called for and technical people wind up in jobs where nontechnical skills are called for. In their book *When Smart People Fail*, Carole Hyatt and Linda Gottlieb strike this nerve:

> Here is a secret about careers: You can get away with unbelievable mistakes if you are socially intelligent. This is the reason why so many mediocre executives survive violent corporate upheavals. Sensitive in their dealings with others, they are genuinely well liked so when they make mistakes, their supporters help them recover. Social intelligence is often far more important to career success than academic brilliance.

If management could thoroughly understand the value of this open secret, the workplace would be much improved. We pay far too little attention to the need for social intelligence (people-skills) in American management which is like selecting an orchestra conductor based on candidates' tuba-playing abilities. The standards of performance imagined by many managers far too often bear little resemblance to the realities of human behavior. Moreover, people with experience, good interpersonal skills, and diplomacy are seen as promotable, regardless of their past educational accomplishments.

At a business seminar not long ago I overheard a conversation in which one party told another that "a college degree in psychology is worthless." The seminar was about total quality management, but the audience and the presenters seemed unaware that the whole premise of such an enterprise rests entirely on an understanding of people. A degree in psychology may be worth little, but knowledge of human psychology is worth a great deal. If this were a well-understood premise, we wouldn't need to attend total quality management seminars. A principle characteristic of successful therapy involves "the personality of the therapist, not the efficacy of theory or dogma."[3] This applies doubly to supervisors and managers. The personality of the supervisor is an essential element to sustained success or failure in any organization.

Management is, after all, the physical manifestation of the power of hierarchy. In her book *Danger in the Comfort Zone*, management consultant Judith M. Bardwick argues that American workers are suffering from an assumption of "entitlement," born of too much security. She contrasts two states of existence within organizations: one of "entitlement" and one of "earning." A state of earning is achieved when an organization is blessed with the right amount of *fear*, which, according to Bardwick, encourages optimum performance. What Bardwick doesn't dwell on, however, is that the responsibility for an attitude of entitlement lies squarely in the court of management. If such a phenomenon exists it is not the fault of workers. When you consider American workers' experience with management strategy for the past 40 years, it is clear where the confusion comes from.

In discussing performance Bardwick makes my point: "A significant reward for excellence of input will be that the ideas get implemented. Publicize people at all hierarchical levels who initiated some new ideas, *who took appropriate risks*" (italics mine). Appropriate risks indeed! Management often reserves for itself the exclusive right to fail, even though everyone knows that the process which produces good ideas also produces bad ideas. In other words, management's historic affection for "doing things right" has applied to employees far more than "doing the right things" which has remained the privileged refuge of management. Success requires some failure, but historically only management has been able to fail without suffering the consequences of failure.

As access to information increases, the right to command is being undermined by subordinates whose recognized contribution is dependent upon transforming data into value. Public information will likely to be used less as a means of control by managers (who use their privilege to information as a substitute for competence) and more by competent employees as a means of encroaching upon traditional authority. Secure, confident managers allow greater access to information to empower workers, but insecure managers are threatened by having workers involved in the knowledge loop. They're inclined to hoard information and use it as a means of controlling the work force. Secure managers understand that a "team" is nothing more than authority redeployed.

Even though the potential for authoritative management still exists and will for years to come, as the competition for competent workers escalates, the need to empower people instead of managing them does also. People who aspire to manage and complain because they lack authority are not yet ready to manage a knowledgeable work force. Knowledge workers must be led and nurtured, not "managed."

Throughout my work experience in large organizations I have watched people engage in off-work hobbies with incredible enthusiasm. Their new field of interest spurs a frenzy of reading and research. They read everything they can find on the subject, talk to everyone who shares their interest who might offer some new angle or insight. But these same individuals, when promoted into management, will often look no further for instruction than to follow the bad examples of managers they themselves have complained about for years.

In the late 1950s, Leon Festinger published *A Theory of Cognitive Dissonance*. In essence, he argued that when too many features of our internal maps of reality are at odds with one another, the need to reduce this dissonance is so strong it becomes a motivating factor in its own right. His book offers this illustration:

> A worker in a factory, for example, may be promoted to the job of foreman. Suddenly he finds himself giving orders instead of receiving them, supervising the work of others instead of being supervised, and the like. Again, these new actions will be dissonant, in many instances, with opinions and values which he acquired as a worker and still holds. In the pursuit of dissonance reduction one would expect this person to quite rapidly accept the opinions and values of the other foreman, that is, opinions and values which are consonant with the things he now does. It would also not be surprising to find that such a person starts seeing less of the workers with whom he used to associate since these workers will not support the changes of opinion which will lead to dissonance reduction. I do not mean to imply that this is a completely sudden change of opinion that occurs or that it is an "all or none" process. Indeed, it may take some time, and some opinions may be very resistant to change so that some dissonance is never eliminated. But the pressure to reduce the dissonance does exist, and a large degree of acceptance of values and opinions appropriate to the new position should be evident.

I have been very fortunate in my own career to have been able to seesaw above and below the management level on many occasions. It's like trying to focus a pair of binoculars on a moving object, but it's a prime exercise in learning to see clearly. And it indelibly impresses upon one's mind the important point that where one stands in relation to management will affect the way one views management, oneself, our economic system and thus reality as a whole.

Knowledge of dealing with others begins with self-awareness, and expertise in management requires at least as much knowledge about human behavior as the specific jobs that need to be done. Managers who do not understand the human dynamics of self-deception, positive illusion, prejudice and the creation of organizational reality mimic the dog that chases its own tail—once the tail is caught, the inexperienced manager, like the dog, is puzzled as to what to do next. The person with a solid understanding of human behavior and knowledge of management history, labor relations and the capabilities of technology, can be an extraordinary manager.

In an August 1994 issue of *Publishers Weekly* magazine, independent journalist Kenneth Lelen used the title "Managing with Soul" to discuss the onslaught of business books in the works which appeal to the brighter side of human relations. It's not surprising that a bloodbath of corporate downsizing would beget a call for soul in management. Whether this search will have any meaningful results in the workplace remains to be seen. The down side of any discussion about soul in the workplace hinges on the fact that it smacks of faddishness. It will be a long time after management has proved possession of a spirit before most of today's workers will pay any attention to chatter about souls. Those of us with old workplace wounds temper our enthusiasm for the latest management craze with dressings of salt to preserve our sanity and our common sense. We've been there. We've heard it all before.

Fortunately, there's evidence that the trends in contemporary management philosophy are becoming increasingly anti-bureaucratic. In *The End of Bureaucracy and the Rise of the Intelligent Organization*, Gifford and Elizabeth Pinchot argue that "today's challenges are too great for bureaucracy and can be met only with self-organizing systems such as free markets, self-rule, and an effective community." Pundits talk of reengineering the corporation, of a focus on process, of networking, and of vital organizations driven by lifelong learning employees. And, make no mistake, these actions combat credentialism. When organizational communications follow patterns which resemble neural networks rather than the traditional vertical channels between supervisors and subordinates—when the knowledge and opinions of individuals in organizations really matter regardless of one's hierarchical standing—then the importance of formal credentials diminish. The growth of democracies and the rising tide of knowledge industries in developing countries are testimony to the anti-bureaucratic value of information at high velocity. In the long term, these forces in and of themselves may contribute significantly to the decredentialing of society.

The Dark Side of Management and Technology

There is a much darker side of management and technology that can appear in any service or industry where knowledge work can be automated. According to Barbara Garson, author of *The Electronic Sweatshop*, the ethos seems to be "automate or be automated." Garson profiles fast-food restaurants, airline reservationists, and stockbrokers to show how workers in these service industry jobs have been stripped of autonomy, initiative, and decision-making ability as their jobs have been reduced to computer programs graded by numbers. Garson writes,

> The goal of modern management—to dictate exactly how a worker does his job and to make him accountable for every minute of the working day—is irrational. It can sometimes be defended in terms of efficiency or productivity, but its only consistent objective is control for the sake of control. That's why any large group of workers who can be automated eventually will be.

Garson's book gives many examples of people whose every move is electronically tabulated, whose telephone calls with customers are monitored and graded by length and whose attempts to close a sale are tallied routinely. This is a sharp contrast to the rosy picture I painted earlier about the opportunities appearing due to the availability of previously hidden information. Management has the prerogative and the wherewithal to use technology as it sees fit. The ultimate evolution of management in a society with a clear division of high-tech versus non-tech work will depend in large part on the availability of both types of workers, and the most lasting decisions may be more political than technical. Sustained draconian working conditions will inevitably lead to a new labor movement.

Automation and Control

In some organizations, as the rate of automation increases, the contempt by management for those actually doing the work increases. The worker is viewed as a functional part, always replaceable by a newer, faster model. The popular cry for excellence is often nothing more than a management call for control, focusing more on how, instead of what and why.

Prior to and during the onset of computer automation I was personally involved in numerous attempts to reduce the actions of the work force to written procedures. The reason given for this activity was to ensure consistency and mobility by allowing anyone to pick up the procedure book and be able to perform that particular job. The process was supposed to guard against the loss of knowledge, but often it produced a far different result. For many workers, the practice of reducing their jobs to specific step-by-step written procedures was equivalent to stripping them of their sense of uniqueness, their ability to add a personal quality to the job. It suggested to them and everyone involved that anyone could do what they were doing. Intended or not, the practice sent a clear message to workers: a lack of respect for individual merit.

It took me a while to realize that reducing a worker's efforts to numbered, sequential activities rarely captures the intuitive expertise developed through years of experience. Indeed there is a natural tendency for workers not to be able to articulate what has been, up to the present, unnecessary to discuss. Sometimes they hold back even if they know. Why should they give away the secret of how to add their special signature of quality to a job?

I used to jump at the chance to participate in these procedure-writing activities because I considered it a challenge and I liked to write. I was often puzzled by the lack of enthusiasm for the project by the other participants. It was a long time before it occurred to me that these procedure-writing frenzies usually corresponded with what might best be described as a loss of control or a feeling of vulnerability on the part of management. This may not have been a conscious assessment on the part of management, but nevertheless the feeling was there. In effect, writing new procedures allowed management to regain management authority by stealing the workers' thunder and subtly demonstrating how unnecessary they were in the first place.

Not everyone in the workplace was demoralized, however. Some seemed to prefer having a simple list of steps to perform as a means of maintaining their distance from their work or protecting themselves by meeting the letter of the law (but no more). These workers were usually in the minority, and their pleasure at being held to simple requirements was usually overshadowed by the loss of autonomy experienced by the majority.

Looking back, I am now convinced that far more harm was done in writing the procedures than if we had just let them go. Moreover, reducing jobs to step-by-step procedures can imply that workers are less important than, and in most cases subordinate to, the computer. This is hardly a way to engender enthusiasm for technology.

If no one is going to watch specifically to see that the written procedures are followed (which wc never did), then they are useless to begin with. If someone is going to watch to see that procedures are followed, you don't need them in writing in the first place. I'm not suggesting that there is anything inherently wrong with written procedures. On the contrary, written procedures are often the foundation of a critical knowledge base. My point is that managers should know when they really need written procedures and when they are just reacting to a perceived lack of control.

Traditional management has historically operated much like a one-way mirror in which the manager is able to observe the workers' performance while remaining protected from scrutiny. In many instances the computer has created a two-way mirror in the workplace. The computer is capable of significantly amplifying the personality of management. Whatever the dominant style of management happens to be, the computer will enhance it. Tyrannical managers can terrorize, creative managers can inspire, and empowering managers can delegate. From a range of authoritative management to a dynamically participative style, the computer allows facilitation to a higher degree—all the more reason to fully understand management's role and how you relate to it specifically.

As long as I can remember, a fundamental notion held deeply by those who profess to manage has been a need to establish and sustain order. When employees complain and gripe, management's reaction is to silence them. Traditional managers assume efficiency by the appearance of order, but order is only evidence of management's ability to exercise control. When employees are speaking out, they are taking the first step toward commitment; they are becoming involved. People who are speaking out are attempting to tell you what they really think, which is but a short distance from showing you what they can really do.

Managers who aspire to "thrive on chaos" cannot expect to measure their success by the appearance of order.[4] There is a loaded paradox here in that few managers know how to cope with an unrestrained, committed work force, especially when the work force is used to being controlled and silenced. Such workers are likely to consider an observable lack of control as evidence of management incompetence, even if everyone in the work force is devoted to doing their best. Harnessing the dynamics of chaos in the workplace requires that managers know as much about management as their employees do about their individual jobs, a task which will replace the one-minute manager with the lifelong learning manager.

Participative Management

For several years "participative management" has been a popular buzzword, but, for reasons already cited, it's had a rough history. Participative management is often announced in an authoritative manner. Subtly or directly the message comes across as, "Everyone will now participate." Rare is the lower-level manager who is not threatened by the idea of sharing power. Rarer still is the work force who does not recognize this as just another ploy to better control their efforts.

Participative management can work—especially in small organizations with few layers of management, where it exists without formal recognition. It is simply the way things are done. But if participative management is to work in organizations with numerous levels of management, nothing less than total commitment is required on the part of upper management and an understanding by everyone involved about what participative management is and what it is not. In his book *Leadership is an Art,* Max De Pree writes, "Participative management arises out of the heart and out of a personal philosophy about people. It cannot be added to, or subtracted from, a corporate policy manual as though it were one more managerial tool." Until recently, failed efforts at participative management have always snapped back toward the centralization of authority. But we are now moving into structural changes that may have a more lasting effect. Downsizing (discussed in Chapter Two) is making participation more desirable in many fields where there has rarely been much opportunity for input from lower-level workers.

Efforts at enlisting participation in traditionally nonparticipative work settings are frequently crude. Sometimes they pose a danger to employees who are genuinely sincere in assisting management in improving overall performance. For example, if management should call everyone together, offer complete amnesty to the group and invite people to state concerns without risk of future retaliation, the wise employee must never, I mean *never*, take this offer seriously. On innumerable occasions I have watched managers make this offer only to have some poor (but sincere) fool accept, pour his or her heart out, and then be the subject of many closed-door meetings called in emergency session to discuss termination strategies. This is not to say that you should not take advantage of opportunities to provide frank input. Just realize that it must be done in private. It is a fundamental hierarchical law to never embarrass your boss in public. Even if traditional boss-subordinate relationships no longer survive in the form of an organizational chart, do not assume the lines of authority have been erased in everyone's mind.

Managers make offers for open communication in the first place because they refuse to admit that they themselves are not above such law. When it represents a sincere effort on the part of management to permanently alter the strategy for performance, participation is unequaled in creating a humanistic workplace. But participative management is very likely to backfire unless everyone on board knows its ultimate aim.

Individual Performance Reviews

Of all of the functions management performs there is nothing in my opinion more destructive than the traditional employee performance review. The performance review is supposed to help establish standards for performance and enable the manager to see that all employees are treated fairly. But, in reality, few managers possess the interpersonal skills to properly handle performance reviews. In most instances, the performance review amounts to an exhibition of power. Like wolves in a pack, employees must display their willingness for subordination.

James R. Fisher calls the American performance appraisal system "the antithesis of quality."[5] This problem is exacerbated by the contradiction of saying, on the one hand, that people should be held accountable for their performance and then, on the other, that we must appreciate the natural differences people bring to the job. Performance needs to be judged continuously, as it occurs, with the respect due a psychologically mature adult. It is more common, however, for managers to save performance reviews as an annual or semiannual ritual, at which time a few gottcha's observed on the run will serve as a formal substitute for guidance and will remain a permanent part of an employee's work record.

Some managers make the best of the review process, but most do not. One could make the argument that performance reviews are efficient, but they are not now, nor have they have they ever been, very effective. Far too often managers who do not recognize the natural (valuable) differences people bring to the workplace use downsizing to minimize differences. This action may appear to set things right, but, in a highly competitive environment, it can amount to the assurance of mediocrity. The employees who are most likely to be let go are the ones who are seen as a threat to present authority. Since these are the people whose stance is usually based upon expertise or critical discourse, it means those who will stay on board rely upon authority by association, which drains knowledge away from the organization. When taken to extreme, all that is left is posture.

This kind of organizational structuring ensures that managers will choose to get rid of the people with whom they most often disagree and keep the people who are more compliant. Moreover, since these are the same people who are in tune with how this manager operates, they will not go all out to produce because they know it is not allowed. They realize that the secret of success in their organization rests on perpetually affirming the authority of the hierarchy. They may be damned agreeable, ready to please, and a real pleasure to work with, but, with little power of their own and little knowledge of how to use it, they will be unable to beat a competitor whose work force is genuinely empowered.

Managing performance, especially in multi-disciplined organizations, is an extraordinarily complicated process made even more difficult by people who underestimate the knowledge and effort required to work effectively with human beings. Almost all of the guidelines for management in America were, and are, designed for the ethos of the power of hierarchy. This is another way of saying we have a long way to go in the field of human resource development.

Above all, people need to feel that they will be rewarded commensurate with their effort. For example, the people in the lower levels of organizations expend as much energy (mental and physical) as the ones in the higher levels, they burn just as many if not more calories of energy on the job, and they go home just as tired, but their salaries or hourly wages do not reflect their efforts. The real expertise and the mystical knowledge is said to be found in the top echelons of management, even if those in power are visibly bungling their jobs. Moreover, the importance of the work carried out in the lower levels of the organization—even if it involves direct contact with the customer—is always downplayed (regardless of any hype about customer relations) in order to justify the great disparity in monetary rewards. Such is the nature of the power of hierarchies. In the olden days of the rising entrepreneur, the saying used to be, "He who has the gold makes the rules." Now, in the modern corporation, where few can even remember who started the business, the saying has changed to, "Whoever has the power uses it."

The appearance of cooperation in a rigid hierarchy tells us little about an organization's potential for performance. During World War Two, prisoners forced to work in Nazi war manufacturing plants found they could reduce production by approximately eighty percent simply by asking for explicit instructions each step of the way.[6] Yet such cooperation in the eyes of the tyrants in charge probably warranted a good performance review.

There are thousands of managers in the workplace today who cut their hierarchical eyeteeth on the ethos of "classical management." As a result, they place little value in the naturally differing ways in which people go about accomplishing their work. They are often fanatically hyperactive about the need for "busyness" (the appearance that everyone is visibly active regardless of whether the task requires action or needs to be carefully thought through). These very managers are apt to walk through their workplace casting an evil eye toward anyone who appears to be idle, but upon reaching their own office will shut the door, prop up their feet, lean back, and try to figure out what to do next. This type of manager is never likely to realize that "teamwork" at its best is a group of people with different strengths switching the role of leadership so fast that no one notices it.

Promotions

In the movie *The Marathon Man*, Sir Laurence Olivier plays a paranoid dentist who was a Nazi during World War Two. As he uses his dental drill to purposely explore the nerves of his captive patient, played by actor Dustin Hoffman, he keeps shouting, "Is it safe? Is it safe?" Hoffman is totally confused with no clue about what this means which results in more drilling and more questions. "Is it safe?" As it turns out, the former Nazi is simply trying to find out if it is safe for him to go to New York to sell some jewels he looted during the war. It would have been perfectly safe were it not for his paranoia.

I present this example to point out a subtle paranoia which often exists below the consciousness of managers in organizations. A very real, very loud, yet not always acknowledged (or not fully thought through) "Is it safe?" drives many organizations. Simply put, this injunction places realistic or at least imaginary pressure on those who want to promote someone to ensure their actions will incur no criticism from superiors about the qualifying criteria for promotion. In other words, to the manager the message is clear: Can I promote this individual without incurring the wrath of those above me? Is it safe? This paranoia may rest on a pile of assumptions which have no basis in fact. Still, American management, in general, has a well-deserved basis for paranoia. It has a miserable record when it comes to making people decisions. Peter Drucker writes:

Executives spend more time on managing people and making people decisions than on anything else, and they should. No other decisions are so long lasting in their consequences or so difficult to unmake. And yet, by and large, executives make poor promotion and staffing decisions. By all accounts, their batting average is no better than .333: at most one-third of such decisions turn out right; one-third are minimally effective; and one-third are outright failures.

In no other area of management would we put up with such miserable performance. Indeed, we need not and should not. Managers making people decisions will never be perfect, of course. But they should come pretty close to batting 1.000, especially because in no other area of management do we know so much.[7]

The pursuit of credentials and the thrust of attempts to obtain credentials is intensified in some organizations by the fact that credentials seem to carry more importance than they really do. For example, managers will often explain that certain individuals were passed over for promotion because they did not have the proper educational credentials, when that isn't the *real* reason at all. It's simply easier to use that excuse than to tell the truth, namely, that in the manager's opinion the person just doesn't measure up or has a personality unsuitable for the work. In such a case, getting a credential while working for the same manager would still not get the person promoted, but it might yield the truth. It's easy to tell the managers who have deep concerns about whether or not their promotion decisions are safe. They are the ones who keep pushing their people to "get that degree" when everyone understands fully there is no relevance, whatsoever, between the degree and job performance.

Most large organizations house a smattering of credentialed incompetents and uncredentialed superstars. This distinction is important because uncredentialed superstars are promoted in much the same way that gifted students are placed in grades higher than their chronological age suggests they should be. This exceptional practice ignores conventional rules in favor of *compelling evidence*, which is precisely what it may take to leap-frog past discrimination barriers.

The dilemmas in today's workplace provide some insight into how the responsibility for human relations is growing throughout our culture. In a competitively focused society, achievement is a distancing mechanism. When there are insufficient ways to judge our accomplishments in comparison to those of others, our history suggests, we are impelled to manufacture them, even if this means resorting to prejudice and bigotry.

Since the publication of *Self-University,* I have been interviewed on radio talk shows coast to coast. One of the most frequent questions I am asked is how to gain a promotion without a degree. That the person seeking the promotion is competent to perform the job is never in doubt, but the lack of a degree is likely to keep the person from ever having an opportunity to get the job or promotion desired. Millions of people face difficulties associated with this problem every day. On one hand, this is a simple problem because it exists in direct proportion to the number of people whose minds must be changed in order to bring about the desired promotion. The larger the organization, the greater the challenge. On the other hand, it is a complex problem because changing minds can be a tall order.

Reflection suggests this is not a credentialing problem so much as it is a cultural problem, a problem of hierarchy. If I am your boss and I know you are competent and deserving of a promotion and yet I fail to promote you because of your lack of a credential that I acknowledge has little if anything to do with the job, the problem is one of custom, of convention, of tradition. Even though these rituals may be easily explained away as having no real value, I may find it extremely difficult to ignore them. How can I be sure the decision I make is safe? If I promote the person I think is the best worker over someone who appears to have more qualifications but whose performance is substandard, I will run the risk of being accused of favoritism. If I promote the qualified but substandard performer, I may be accused of being blind. Why is the better qualified person doing poorly? Why is the less qualified person performing better? In dynamic progressive organizations the reasons for promotions are clear and fair. How one performs in the present takes precedence over past accomplishments.

A primary reason for so much difficulty in matters of promotional policy is that, in spite of evidence to the contrary, it is still generally accepted as common sense that good grades, degrees, and certificates will mean good performance. A superior level of traditional education, however, does not guarantee better performance. In fact, some studies suggest the reverse. For a myriad of jobs that have been studied, including insurance salesmen, air traffic controllers, secretaries, technicians, clerks, and factory workers (both male and female), high school graduates consistently performed better than workers with college degrees.[8] Moreover, the same studies also showed that, as educational level increases, so does job dissatisfaction, leading to more frequent changes of employment—"evidence that education may be primarily regarded as a matter of status by those who possess it."[9]

There is also a long-held assumption on the part of employers that says a person with a degree, even in a field unrelated to the one at hand, will somehow have more to offer than anyone with experience in the field but no degree. After years of accepting the general premise that a classroom environment is necessary before learning takes place, we still cling to such fallacies even in the face of contrary evidence. In his book *The Credential Society*, Randall Collins argues that, where the acquisition of technical skills is concerned, the "educationocracy is mostly bureaucratic hot air" rather than a producer of real technical skills. Most technical skills are learned today the same way they were learned two hundred years ago: on the job.

The notion that higher learning is totally dependent on institutions or even instruction is ludicrous. The real tragedy is that people attend learning institutions primarily for the wrong reasons. If most people went to college because of an authentic thirst for knowledge, we would have the capability and impetus for profoundly changing our own lives and our society for the better. Many people go to graduate school because of a soft job market—a stinging indictment of bona fide inquiry. How unfortunate that millions are drawn to universities not by an insatiable desire for knowledge but rather by the strongly felt need to distance oneself from others economically. It is a well-demonstrated myth that formal education necessarily improves people. Send a jerk to college and you produce a jerk who will now feel legitimacy for being that way.

Traditional education is the root of a subtle but persistent message that form is more important than substance, appearance more important than reality. When this is translated into "street smarts" it suggests that the real reason for classroom effort is not so much to learn as it is to establish ranking among students. If you don't believe this, try to convince the parents of A students that doing away with the grading system would make learning a more intrinsically rewarding activity.

Further, our system of formal education reinforces the notion that the only avenue to success is to be found in the demonstration of academic skills. My workplace observations, however, suggest something else. The reason most people fail in organizations is not from a lack of academic or technological knowledge, but a lack of understanding about how to get along well with other people, a subject that, for all practical purposes, is totally overlooked in traditional education.

Technology and structural changes are adding a downward pressure by eliminating the need for mid-level jobs precisely when large numbers of babyboomers in the work force expect to be promoted. The promotion ladder in established organizations is becoming increasingly crowded at just the wrong time. Resentment is building because the babyboom generation grew up believing that good work is rewarded and recognition is achieved by climbing the organizational ladder. One of management's self-perpetuating problems stems from the ethos of the organizational ladder itself. James R. Fisher writes, "Organizational climbers are incapable of leading. They have been schooled to react to situations, not to create them."[10]

The nature of competition is so fierce in our society that we have an acute need for a tremendous number of losers. Second to the financial standing of one's parents, academic status defines one's ranking in the social hierarchy. This is how we keep score of who is better than whom. Sometimes this phenomenon is very subtle, sometimes not. A few months ago I recall a social scandal in the news brought about because a debutante married a house painter. Now, a debutante is simply a young (upper class) woman making a formal entrance into society, but a house painter is finished by the implication that he can never rise above what he does for a living. He is after all "just a house painter." College students who drive delivery trucks to work their way through school are viewed as students, but a person who drives a delivery truck and does not attend college is, in time, "just a truck driver" and becomes stereotyped as such. This pigeonholing is so pervasive I have formulated the *white knight theory* to explain why so few people are promoted in the companies for which they are already working.

White Knight Theory

Simply stated, the white knight theory says we have been educationally conditioned to expect more from the unknown than from the known and, in particular, more from the process of formal education than the system delivers. Consciously and subconsciously managers stereotype employees, limiting them to the functions which they already perform and failing to consider potential in those same individuals for performing work no one seems to be doing. But out there somewhere, the belief is, will be someone who possesses the necessary skills and who will perform so well that the reasons for the hiring decision will be immediately obvious to everyone. Capable, competent employees in the American workplace are routinely passed over for promotion because they do not fit the mental image held by their superiors of what the person filling the vacant position should be like. It is truly a baffling paradox. They may be asked to fill positions on a temporary basis until such time that the white knight is hired. They may perform superbly and may even be expected to train the white knight, but the common belief is these individuals are incapable of continuing to perform the job indefinitely.

Often people just out of college are hired into what's known as the "fast track," meaning that they are expected to rise quickly in the ranks of their organization. They are often called management trainees; some are talented, some are not. Though I've watched this process on numerous occasions, I don't recall a single instance in which someone hired for the fast track was better qualified or better suited than someone who was already in the workplace, but who lacked the distinction of being recognized as "promotable." To promote a white knight is a "safe" management decision.

Affirmative Action and Discrimination

My position on affirmative action has changed 180 degrees over the past decade. I used to be adamantly opposed to the idea that a wrong can be set right by yet another wrong, but I have come to realize that the reason we need affirmative action for dark-skinned people today is that for more than two centuries we had affirmative action for light- skinned people, except nobody had to legislate it, talk about it or even acknowledge it. It was simply considered self-evident just a few decades ago that white people were superior to other races; obviously they deserved the lion's share of opportunities. Now, the expectation that, because we know better today, we can simply stop the racial bigotry and discrimination that resulted from these long-held assumptions is totally absurd. Human nature does not work this way. Ingrained opinions assumed during early socialization are incredibly difficult to alter. Two wrongs don't make a right, but a remedy born of a resolution to make amends for past injustices, is certainly a more positive action than the deep-seated opression which resulted from the wrongs of racial hatred and bigotry in the first place.[11] James Fallows writes, "The caste system in India is a form of private action against competition, since it excludes most people from certain jobs. Prejudice against minority groups has the same effect."[12]

It's very hard to appreciate the power of beliefs, especially beliefs we hold just below everyday consciousness. Ellen J. Langer demonstrates the force of this type of belief in her book *Mindfulness:*

> Moisten your mouth with your saliva—the back of your teeth, the tip of your tongue, and so on. It should feel pleasant. Now spit some saliva into a clean glass. Finally, sip a small bit of this liquid back into your mouth. Disgusting, isn't it? Why? For a number of reasons, we learned years ago that spitting is nasty.

Even when there is no sensible reason for the body to feel re-pelled, the old mindset prevails.

This same cast of mind applies to all of the beliefs you and I have acquired as the result of our socialization. It is not any easier to rid our minds of learned prejudice than it is to change our attitude toward evacuated spittle. This is why public discussion about ghetto schools focuses on low achievement and inferior students, but when low achievement occurs in better neighborhoods the focus changes to poor instruction. The need for affirmative action will end when talent and ability are recognized for what they are, irrespective of an individual's gender, race, religion, social standing, or paper tickets.

Gender and Glass Ceilings

We've seen that job performance cannot be measured accurately on the basis of school grades, even though our system operates as if it were literally true. But there is an interesting paradox associated with this phenomenon. Studies reveal that, other things being equal, women get better grades in almost every field of study, and yet this supposed performance indicator does not show up in their salaries.

Moreover, it is common knowledge that women face invisible barriers to promotion and career advancement which have nothing whatsoever to do with academic achievement, learned competence, or natural ability. If this were not true, how could we explain the practice of pretending to estimate achievement through grades and then ignoring the evidence? These impediments to economic equality arise from the power of hierarchy. They reside in what may be called unconscious assumptions, or a form of special "common sense," on the part of those who create the barriers. The pervasiveness and tenacity of such rigid thinking stems from the fact that all of us can easily see the unwarranted "prejudicial" thinking of others, but find it extremely difficult to detect our own.

Gender bias is clearly the reason secretarial jobs stopped being considered apprenticeships for management: an attitude which was adopted in the late nineteenth century when women began taking secretarial positions formerly held by men.[13] The history of the salaries of working women in America demonstrates clearly how hard it is to change behavior simply because of a new intellectual awareness. The salaries of women working in comparable jobs with men have gained some ground in recent years, but a huge discrepancy in pay equity remains. Why is this still true? Why does a woman with a college degree earn roughly the same as a man of the same age with only a high school diploma? Don't we know better than this? Why do women with credentials and the competence to back them up, repeatedly fail to reach the top of their chosen fields? There is much more at work here than common sense. These inequities are clearly a product of pyramid power.

This picture of predominating management practices isn't pretty. Indeed, facing the bulwark of long-held organizational beliefs and traditions—now varnished with the effects of downsizing, automation, and ever subtler forms of discrimination—how can a competent person without the magic tickets hope to get ahead? Understanding the context is at least half the battle. Let's take a look at how credentials come to be established and accepted.

Chapter Four

Understanding Credentialing Methods

By creating a belief in their own knowledge as objective experience, and helping to organize schooling and the division of labor to suit their own ends, professionals have essentially turned modern knowledge into private property. As in Mandarin China, such intellectual property is becoming the coin of the realm, convertible into class power, privilege and status.

—Charles Derber

Guilds and Professional Associations

It is a noble effort to try to ensure against malpractice of any type. No one wants to have their trust compromised by people who claim skills they do not have. Unfortunately, something always seems to go awry when groups attempt to establish standards of performance in order to protect the public from injury. What happens is a product of the power of hierarchy, namely, that the members of the these well-meaning groups almost never hold themselves accountable for high standards. Instead they focus on limiting entry into the group. They create a maze of arbitrary hurdles and obstacles the novice will have to survive in order to be afforded the franchise of the guild. The group members' certificates, degrees, or licenses will likely do more to keep their services from scrutiny than it will to afford the public high levels of service. A medical license will tenure a doctor for life, regardless of whether or not he or she continues to keep pace with research and the information explosion in medicine.

I would rather see a statement providing evidence of a surgeon's success ratio of operations performed than a framed medical license on the wall (which former U.S. Surgeon General C. Everett Koop has referred to as "outcomes research"), but the power of hierarchy prevents this. Some health care critics have estimated that more people die each year through quackery and malpractice than from all acts of violent crime, and yet most of the culpable practitioners still have a license to practice.[1] I frequently use examples from the medical field to illustrate problems with credentialing, not to pick on doctors, but because of the enormous trust we place in them, their capacity to abuse that privilege, and the pyramid power used to squelch awareness of abuse.

Media frequently spotlight bizarre incidents of malpractice, but the public perception is managed well enough to keep the problems seemingly small compared to those of violent crime. If we pay attention, we will notice a multitude of warnings from all types of associations and institutions about the importance of finding the "right doctor" for a particular illness or disease. The same caveat applies to hiring a lawyer.[2] But if it is not to save us from some type of harm, why are these warnings necessary? If something is not deeply wrong in the field of medical practice, then why is there so much dialogue about the need to get "a second opinion?" The general public considers medical practice to be science, but physicians understand it as an art. We are partially oblivious to negative information in the field of medicine because we do not want it to be true. Have you noticed how everyone who is going to be operated on almost always claims to have found the best surgeon in their particular part of the country to perform the surgery? The faith necessary to allow a total stranger to cut open one's body must rest upon extreme trust.

A surgeon and lecturer at the Harvard School of Public Health, Lucian L. Leape, has been quoted as saying, "Medical injury is indeed a hidden epidemic." Dr. Leape estimates:

> More than 1.3 million hospitalized Americans—nearly one in 25—are injured annually by medical treatment. About 100,000 people—one in 400 patients—die each year as a direct result of such injuries... more than twice the annual death toll on the nation's highways.[3]

This is not welcome news. The reality of Dr. Leape's assertions is not accepted as common knowledge by the general public nor is it likely to be in the near future, simply because such knowledge poses too great a threat to public security. And yet, the soaring costs of malpractice insurance are not born solely of greedy patients trying to "cash in" from unfortunate circumstances. There is a significant amount of medical malpractice which is exacerbated by the very structure of our system of qualification: the license to practice medicine grants a physician the right to engage in malpractice until he or she dies.

Guilds established in the name of public safety do far more to guarantee the earning potential of physicians than they do to save the public from poor quality health care. They provide more protection for members than for the public. They always have and they always will. I don't mean to imply that there are not people in such associations who genuinely have the public interest at heart. But those who do are themselves often likely to underestimate "the power of hierarchy" preserved by guilds and associations.

A convincing piece of evidence about the tendency of guilds to place a higher priority over the guardianship of their members than the welfare of the public is suggested by the fact that, although medical school is exceedingly hard to get into, almost no one ever flunks out.[4] The medical profession represents the pinnacle of the credentialed world, but credentialism is itself much like a disease—it spreads too easily.

The American educational system is another case in point. Many professors become so obsessed with their comparative professional standings that they squabble constantly with their colleagues, not about the value of ideas, but over who thought of them first. They reduce their ability to create value by focusing on technique instead of on the underlying principles they set out to discover. Educational institutions are especially susceptible to the power of hierarchy because of the practice of tenure. Educator Stephen D. Brookfield has written that, "When a large grant is awarded by a foundation or corporation to a college or university, the scramble by departments and individuals to obtain pieces of this sometimes makes Machiavelli seem fainthearted and overly scrupulous."[5] But this scramble is a mild reaction compared to what happens when someone challenges the franchise on knowledge held by a group of educators. Sharks attacking raw meat couldn't capture the frenzy.

A further side effect of the guild mentality is that any member who dares to speak or write in a way the general public can understand becomes subject to ridicule and likely to pick up a pejorative title as well. For example, instead of just being psychologists, they become "pop" psychologists. After all, if the general public is able to understand what is intended as an esoteric knowledge franchise, then the value of that knowledge may be threatened. Yes, it's appropriate to use the term "pop psychology" to discredit half truths based upon mixtures of science and popular public opinion, but not when the work simply explains in plain words what has become unnecessarily mysterious.

In spite of the rhetoric about universal education, academics preserve their canon of make-believe absolute truth through an alliance of cryptic language. It is not *meant* to be understood by the general public. As the authors of *Power in the Highest Degree* explain, "Rather, it is couched in language designed to cultivate the myth that professional knowledge is too complex and esoteric for the untutored to understand. This inspires awe and discourages nonprofessionals from trying to educate themselves."[6]

The Psychology of Commitment

Credentials include high school diplomas, college degrees, certificates, licenses, and a myriad of different types of documentation that attest to ability. In many fields, whether or not a formal guild exists, educational credentials seem to represent evidence of commitment rather than evidence of guaranteed competence. This is especially true in the case of a high school diploma, because the completion of high school is considered by most employers merely as an intermediate step in the long process of qualification. Failure to complete high school means one's ability to fit minimum social and academic standards is immediately suspect.

Indeed, many prospective employers will assume that a lack of commitment to finish high school is caused by a character flaw which would make such a person an unacceptable risk as an employee. When a job applicant is anywhere from 18 to 25 years old, there is a sharp focus on the part of the potential employer to ask for evidence of a high school diploma. Applicants who are past that "risky" age group are better off to choose other proof of qualification than to try seeking a diploma so late. Returning to school for the diploma when one is obviously too old puts unnecessary focus on a deficiency which could go unnoticed by most employers unless brought to their attention.

The psychology of commitment turns the table from professional associations to associations among professionals which means, once members have the power to hire others, they will choose among their own alumni. The psychology of commitment derives from the simple observation that overt positive action reinforces commitment. In other words, when we take action in a particular activity we increase our commitment to that activity as a result. This is the principle advertisers use when they ask us to enter contests by simply writing the name of their product on a form before we send it in. They know that this process will increase our sense of commitment to their product, if for no other reason than to reduce our embarrassment at having participated in a foolish task.

Now consider how the effort required to go through four years of college (or any qualifying activity) must increase a student's commitment to the current system of qualification. Even if there are absolutely no connections between the degree and the job sought, the degree holder is likely to feel that he or she should have first consideration for hiring or promotion simply because commitment to the system of qualification has been demonstrated. Paradoxically this sense of entitlement becomes true for most people who know that their process of qualification is arbitrary, and that it has nothing to do with their actual performance. Having gone through the qualification process, even though they knew it wasn't necessary, they now become adamant supporters of the arbitrary system. In this light, it's easy to see how change-resistant our antiquated system of qualification is, not to mention the economic interest our educational institutions have in seeing that the system remains intact.

Studies have shown repeatedly that there is little correlation between grades and lifetime achievement, although the inference is continually made that it's a given.[7] College attendance and career success are linked more by the fact that a diploma will produce more opportunities to learn occupational skills on the job than the fact that college graduates are inherently better performers. And, in spite of the fact that almost everyone with years of workplace experience knows this, the psychology of commitment is likely to surface among large numbers of people who have— at least in their own minds—"paid their dues." For the rest of their lives they are likely to see themselves as superior in intellect to those who did not attend college, even when its obvious to everyone else that they aren't.

Registration, Certification, Licensure

The simplest form of credentialing is registration. Registration for an occupation is very similar to registration for an automobile, except that character references may be required and bonding may be used instead of collision insurance. The fundamental advantage of registration is that it affords interested parties the ability to identify the person or object registered. Certification, on the other, hand attests to a certain level of exposure or competence and may allow the person certified exclusive use of a title. The title may be limited to a specific organization such as a training school. Certification restricts the use of the title, but not the occupational field. For example, someone can be a mechanic without being certified, but, to be a certified Ford mechanic, that person might have to attend a Ford training school.

The next credentialing step is licensure, which restricts occupational practice to only those who have the license. To obtain a license one may be required to demonstrate skills, pass a test, or attend years of schooling, as in the case of a medical doctor. In 1987, 643 occupations in the United States required registration, 65 required certification, and 490 required licensure.[8]

The most common experience the majority of us have with licensure is the requirement for a license to drive an automobile. And here again, even though our efforts are well intentioned, we are not very good at screening out bad drivers who are able at one time or another to muster the skills necessary to fool a driving instructor. And failure to pass a written driving test doesn't necessarily mean someone is not a good driver. On more than one occasion as a police officer I was outrun in a high-speed chase by someone who turned out to be barely literate, but who could drive like Mario Andretti.

In his book *The Rule of Experts*, S. David Young wrote,

> Occupational regulation has served to limit consumer choice, raise consumer costs . . .deprive the poor of adequate services, and restrict job opportunities for minorities—all without a demonstrated improvement in quality or safety of the licensed activities.

The distinction of respectability afforded to those who are certified has prompted a rise of certified astrologers, psychics, and channelers whose claim to cryptic knowledge rests upon the gullibility of the public. In this sense, credentialism fuels the placebo effect. People who use the services of certified and licensed charlatans often believe they have been well served because of their faith in professionalism, when, in fact, they have been fleeced.

Grades, Testing, and Success

Atlantic Monthly editor, James Fallows, has examined differences in the way Americans and the Japanese view academic achievement. In *More Like Us*, Fallows remarks,

> In Japan, passing tests and getting into the right schools are more important than in America, but the idea of ultimate ability seems to matter less. When someone does poorly on a university entrance exam, he doesn't necessarily tell himself he's stupid. He and his parents are more likely to say, "Pass with four, fail with five!"—referring to hours of sleep the candidate is allowed each night while cramming for another try at the exams. Such effort would be pointless if the tests were thought to measure raw ability. But the Japanese assumption is that just about everybody has "enough" ability; what the tests really

measure is determination. Therefore, students have a reason to try their best. American IQ and Scholastic Aptitude Tests convey the opposite message: Don't worry about cramming, students. This is a measure of the real you.

Where did Americans get the idea that there were precise, innate, very important differences in ability, which could be used to direct people to the right role in adult life? Partly it came from the universal human impulse to put people into hierarchies and to prove that whatever hierarchy exists is fair.

Fallows strikes a nerve that may allow us to gain some insight into why the issue of effort and merit is so confusing. A good case could be made that Americans should pay more attention to effort and the Japanese should take a stronger look at natural ability. Effort and natural ability deserve attention, but how either country ever came to believe that a comprehensive education is necessary for only a few of its citizens is a notable mystery. True, there are only so many well-paying jobs to be found in either culture, but the quality of life in each country is synergistically connected to the educational level of its citizens.

In America, we often confuse opportunity with determination. We view the effort the child uses to ride the bicycle as evidence of deserving the bicycle. In Japan, the culture of conformity is so strong that individual affinities are essentially ignored. Thus, people who try hard enough can land jobs for which they are not well suited. This happens in America, too, but more so in Japan. The result is that the Japanese work force frequently appears near a nervous breakdown. It is not uncommon in Japan for people to work themselves to death. Again, this happens in America, too, but in Japan they have a special name for the condition: karoshi. In America we pay far too little attention to the workers who expend extraordinary effort on the job while we wait for those with suspected natural ability to become inspired and perform. Both cultures waste productivity by creating unnecessary stress for their workers.

On another level, it is important to observe that being motivated by grades is not related to a thirst for knowledge. Moreover, there is little doubt that extrinsic rewards reduce intrinsic satisfaction.[9] In effect, grades have become the purpose of education. People search for approval instead of knowledge; when the grades stop, so does their inquiry. Indeed, a large part of the conceit upon which the power of a hierarchy depends—and in fact feeds—is the desire to please others. James R. Fisher writes, "There is no single tendency in the American psyche that causes more frustration and loss of purposefulness than the insane drive to Please Others."[10]

Study after study shows that good grades are not a reliable indicator of anything but predicting good grades; they do not predict good workplace performance. Psychologist David McClelland spent many years studying why people succeed and others do not. His findings are not popular with academia. He writes, "It seems so self-evident to educators that those who do well in their classes *must* go on to do better in life that they systematically have disregarded evidence to the contrary that has been accumulating for some time."[11] In his 1961 book *The Achieving Society*, McClelland attributed successful achievement to what he characterized as the *n Achievement factor* which I interpret as sort of a residue of cultural expectation about how much control one has over one's life. McClelland argued that a more appropriate enterprise than making predictions based on grades in school would be examining "grades in life."[12]

A large measure of our self-esteem depends upon our definition of intelligence and how we apply it to ourselves. Our educational system implies we can deduce ability through the use of grades and testing. In spite of Charles Murray's and Richard J. Herrnstein's controversial assertions about intelligence in their book *The Bell Curve*, arguments by people such as physicist Phillip Morrison of MIT, biologist Stephen J. Gould, educator Howard Gardner of Harvard, Michael Olneck of the University of Wisconsin, James Crouse of the University of Delaware and many others, cause me to believe that IQ is to intelligence as a thermometer is to room temperature. It merely reflects the environment or degree of stimulation which the subject has experienced and no more. In other words, judging people solely on the basis of IQ as a reliable indicator of their potential is like rescuing frying eggs from a skillet to judge the heat they have attained relative to their capacity to cook. Even the brightest humans never exhaust their brain power. The human brain is capable of complex reorganization, even during old age. Through continuous learning we are able to break through to new levels of understanding, to new revelations which place all that we already know in a completely new light. Testing is a natural "human" activity that we are instinctively drawn to. We go to incredible lengths to test our emotional limits.

Testing is a vital way to judge what remains to be taught, but the way testing is typically used tends to destroy individuals' thirst for knowledge. Test scores have no way of indicating what we might learn or ultimately discover. Albert Einstein's teachers concluded from his tests that he was not college material, but his theories about relativity revolutionized the world of science. Thomas Edison was thought to be stupid because he did not adapt well to school, but his work transformed the way we live. Charles Darwin was thought to be ill-suited to academics and therefore not smart enough to become a doctor, but his work as a naturalist forever changed how we see ourselves as human beings in relation to the rest of world. The Wright brothers did not attend college, but, if they had, they would have failed tests on scientific principles about whether or not man could build a machine that could fly. What is the value of testing which suggests that thinkers like these do not really belong in the educational system? These individuals shared a burning desire to know, a strong desire to be self-determining. They knew intuitively what direction to take, what to study next. They developed their own curricula. They did not have to be pushed to study. On the contrary, they were pulled toward discovery and were so curious that they refused to be distracted by rote learning.

What does it mean when people who don't or won't follow the standard packaged curriculum are regarded as different from the rest of us? Why must it be bizarre behavior which results in inventions like electricity, light bulbs, phonographs, and airplanes? An educational process that seems determined to keep students from developing their own ideas is bound to be regarded with skepticism by those subject to it.

The acceptance of cheating by so many students in order to pass in college appears to be supported, in part, by the unconscious belief that many tests, and maybe even some of the courses, are irrelevant. If the material doesn't matter, the thinking goes, then cheating won't either. The concept of "cheating" reveals a fundamental flaw in the way students are "taught." In his book *Doing Philosophy*, Thomas Ellis Katen addresses the idea of cheating:

> A student may cheat by deviously gazing at another student's paper or at carefully secreted cue cards, and then writing what he learns there on his paper, passing it off as his own work. Many administrators and teachers regard this as immoral, and some have sought to trap cheaters as if they were criminals on the Most Wanted List. Honest students are those who stay up all night diligently memorizing what someone else wrote in a textbook. The next day these students come in and carefully write down what they remember from their reading last night. What they write down is something copied from someone else's work, too, but the difference is that the diligent students remember what they copy for a few hours longer than the cheaters.

Students and teachers who believe consciously or subconsciously that what they are doing is not really important are tacitly saying that investing time that way beats figuring out what *is* important. Such an effort might reveal what many suspect, but would not want to admit: The existing system is designed to perpetuate the status quo. David Owen, author of *None of the Above*, wrote, "Tests like the SAT convert the tainted advantages of birth and wealth onto the neutral currency of merit, enabling the fortunate to believe they have earned what they have merely been given."

About our system of merit Owen continues:

> In American society, "merit" is usually little more that camouflage for class. Through a meritocratic sleight of hand, society's rewards become their own justification: if the meritocracy is supposed to reward the worthy by giving them high salaries, then people with high salaries must be worthy. The rich must be smart; how else did they get so rich? And the poor, of course, must be dumb.

Accepted views about testing resurface in the arena of credentials and the workplace. In school you will be given time to study for a test. The same time allowance for preparation also applies to most situations in the workplace when you're asked to do something for the first time. But the inexperienced credential holder will be expected by many to be able to immediately perform the task as a result of having earned the credential (there is an implied connection here, but it may have no basis in fact), even though it may be the first time anyone has performed this task. Such a situation sets up the uncredentialed to believe that, even though they themselves continually are able to rise to these occasions, they are nevertheless unqualified for lack of credentials. Too often they view the successful efforts of others to be a result of an education while they see themselves as simply muddling through.

Degrees

In her book *The Case Against College,* Caroline Bird offers a precise, common-sense approach to determining whether or not you should attend college. All you have to do is multiply your projected annual income by the number of years you have left to work, then add up the cost of attending college and subtract it from the projected income you would receive if you had the degree you are seeking. This simple formula raises some complex questions. First of all, it's not as simple as it seems, because to complete this exercise you must figure in how much interest the money spent to go to college would have earned if it had simply stayed in a savings account. The dynamics of compounded interest are staggering: if you take the tuition amount to attend any college at age 18 and then figure out what the account would accrue over the next 47 years to age 65, the total will dwarf your workplace earnings.

This fact brings up some strange notions about the way we attribute economic value to human beings. For example, when going to college isn't economically feasible, a person can probably get a loan to go to school. However, if that same person needed a medical operation simply to survive, loan money would be scarce.

Bird's book was published in 1975, and, although her premise is still valid, some aspects of work and income have changed dramatically. Downsizing and global competition are contributing to a sharp rift between good-paying and low-wage jobs. Still, economic success, important as it may be, is not the sole point of life, nor is it the only element of consequence in work. If challenging, interesting work is important to your sense of fulfillment, then a college degree may be worthwhile, even if paying for it does not make very good economic sense. Nevertheless, it is contrary to purpose that today in America college degrees sought solely for the sake of job qualification are in themselves rarely good indicators of what field a person is likely to wind up working in.

Chapter Five

Who is Really Qualified?

Perhaps there is no idea about human learning harder to accept for people familiar with classroom schools than this: that the ideal of neat, orderly, closely planned, sequentially logical teaching will in practice, with young students, guarantee severe learning failure for most.

—Leslie A. Hart

Education and Credentials

The reality of the world of credentials is that one can be over-qualified for a particular job, yet not even be seen as a candidate. So how do we know who is really qualified? How do we know which person should be hired or promoted over someone else? This is a complex proposition on one hand, but not so difficult to determine on the other. It is hard to criticize traditional education in the manner that I do without being misunderstood, especially when I imply that college is not necessary as a prerequisite for many specific jobs and occupations. I am not suggesting that *knowledge* is not necessary. On the contrary, I'm saying that higher education's external push to qualify people for jobs often inhibits the very learning necessary for enabling knowledge and developing competence. Knowledge, not college, is what we need in the workplace and in our personal lives.

Place a small child in a new culture where a different language is spoken, and not one word will be required to induce the child to learn the new language. Language acquisition will simply happen as a consequence of long-term interaction and exposure. But sit down with a child and explain that you are going to teach a new language, and you may decide you'd rather wrestle an alligator. The same principle applies to the workplace. Most of us learn our jobs while on the job, not in the classroom. This realization should cause some doubt as to the wisdom of using the classroom experience as the most significant qualifying factor for employment opportunities.

The history of American experience offers clear evidence in all phases of human accomplishment that people are at their best, competently and creatively, when they follow their own intuition and proceed at their own pace. Yet our educational system functions as if it purposely sets out to defy this truth. We have fashioned educational factories to mass-produce learning as if each student were an identical product to every other. For decades we have approached education as if the class were more important than the student, as if there were no students—simply a class to be taught. We have always known that learning is a personal endeavor, but traditional education sacrifices the individual for the sake of the group. Individual students must deaden their intellect in order to proceed at a group pace. The fourth-grade student excited about twelfth-grade astronomy is restrained. The twelfth-grade student having difficulty with fourth-grade math is humiliated. The impact of this external, group-centered, grade-centered enterprise is that, for millions of students, it dampens the flame of curiosity or extinguishes it altogether.

Extrinsic rewards diminish the intrinsic satisfaction for performing a particular task by subtly implying that the task is not worthwhile for its own sake. Our educational system favors an extrinsic approach when, beyond any doubt, the *intrinsic* value of education is the greatest requisite for any recipient to wish to continue pursuing it. Not surprisingly, then, for the majority of students, education becomes a dreaded activity, and for others it becomes the art of demonstrating good behavior rather than an enterprise to be pursued for its own sake. Ubiquitous use of the term "over-educated" implies that education exists for technique alone. Students learn exceedingly well that rewards, like good paying jobs, are desirable. Achieving good grades, they believe, will earn them the right to such jobs. But a great many of these same people will not continue to study throughout their lives because they have been taught that an education is something that can be gotten out of the way.

This is the most destructive message picked up by students in our educational system: that an education is something which must be endured and dispensed with as quickly as possible. Further, if the education costs a lot of money, it will lead to high earnings. The result of this absurdity is that individuals pursue an education for every conceivable reason under the sun except to really become educated. The student does not set out to master. Each class, each test, each activity is simply a means to get to the next one, and to eventually meet a requirement. Grudgingly going through the motions (as do many college students I've observed), and wading through a series of classes while maintaining little interest other than getting by, have little more long-term learning benefit than simply going to the movies—maybe less. Ronald Dore, author of *The Diploma Disease,* has said the following about qualifications:

> In the process of qualification . . . the pupil is concerned not with mastery, but with being certified as having mastered. The knowledge that he gains, he gains not for its own sake and not for constant later use in a real life situation—but for the once-and-for-all purpose of reproducing it in an examination. And the learning and reproducing is all just a means to an end—the end of getting a certificate which is a passport to a coveted job, a status, an income. If education is learning to *do* a job, qualification is a matter of learning in order to *get* a job.
>
> The difference is a difference in what is now fashionably called the "hidden curriculum." What the educator is saying implicitly—and sometimes explicitly—to his pupils is: "learn this or you will not become a good doctor, a skillful carpenter, a fully-developed human being, a good useful citizen; you will not know how to *earn* your living, you will not be able to appreciate the higher pleasures of art or poetry." What the qualifier says to his pupils is: "learn this or you will not get the chance to be a doctor or a carpenter; nobody will *give* you a living." The first appeals to the inner standards of conscience and promises self-achieved fulfillment; the second invokes external arbiters, threatens exclusion, evokes anxiety. The first preserves the teacher-pupil relation as complete in itself; the second makes both dependent on the tyranny of the examiners.

Now, to this emphasis on qualification add the fact that we spend almost no time in traditional education trying to discover our own individual talents and how they differ from the talents of others. Moreover, we compound the problem by making no real connection between our talents (because at this point we don't know what they are) and the traits required to perform day-to-day jobs in the workplace. Knowing unhesitatingly what your strengths are is the backbone of confidence.

As I've written elsewhere, there's evidence all around that people may be good at earning a living but not at *living* a living. To squander an education for the sole purpose of acquiring credentials is equivalent to eating for the sole purpose of gaining weight. Malnourishment will likely result from either effort.

Traditional education is not all bad. There are many students who thrive on the system the way it is, just as there are many colleges and universities that offer education of real value. Some courses available are specifically applicable to the workplace. Indeed, the existence of colleges and universities stems from the noblest of human aspirations; the campus can be a wonderful place. But I believe it is morally indefensible that the majority of people who attend institutions of higher learning do so for external reasons which have little to do with the quality of the experience itself. Instead of a brief four-year blitz encounter, we should depend upon and use colleges and universities throughout our lives. Moreover, we are decidedly better able to learn and gain from new knowledge when we have a rich repertoire of experience with which to contrast our learning.

In this book, I am most concerned with the many kinds of work which can be (and are) learned on the job by people who can read, write, use general math, think critically, and creatively, and who can ask the right questions and find the right answers themselves. There is currently a great deal of criticism from business leaders about the uneducated work force and the advanced skills required to meet the demands of the future. Many of these criticisms are valid because, in our ambivalence to deal with credentialism effectively, we have created a monolithic credentialing bureaucracy. "In a bureaucracy 'realism' means doing nothing this year too markedly inconsistent with what was done last year. If it was done last year, it is 'our policy,' and no matter how inane and unsuccessful it might have proven, flying in the face of it becomes 'unrealistic.'"[1] To ensure the creation of bureaucracy in any type of organization, all one has to do is limit the discretion of the participants so that their authority is not greater than the function of nuts and bolts. The major point missed by most of the people who really need to understand is that bureaucracy is a product of hierarchy. The taller the hierarchical pyramid, the greater the rigidity of the bureaucracy. Perhaps the main reason we fail to take drastic measures to change this situation is that we have not yet figured out what type of a process should be put in its place.

I don't profess to have all of the answers to solving this problem, but the place to start seems profoundly obvious. We must stop denying our own experience. Regardless of how we try to measure merit and achievement, we must reserve the right to recognize both excellence and incompetence when we see them and to act accordingly. We know without any doubt that degrees and certificates do not guarantee competence and that many skills requiring them are learned on the job, not in the classroom. Moreover, because we know this, it also follows that putting too much emphasis on qualification and too little on the actual demonstration of competence means we are loosing value by a clear abdication of responsibility. We are giving authority to institutions that do not deserve it.

A person with a degree may have any number of motivations for obtaining it and deserves recognition and respect for having the persistence to complete it. If the degree really stands for knowledge, and if the knowledge is relevant to the tasks at hand, then the person should have a decisive competitive advantage. Like everyone else in the workplace, this individual should be given an opportunity to demonstrate applicable knowledge and skills. But those who fail in performance should not be given a blanket benefit of the doubt because they have credentials which fail to bespeak their actual experience. In other words, they should not be allowed a franchise for incompetence which denies those with the right skills the opportunity to demonstrate them, regardless of how those skills were obtained.

American business organizations would be far more efficient, effective, competitive, and dynamic, if the educational histories of all employees were expunged from personnel records immediately upon hire and were never spoken of again. Then, if an individual's schooling had in reality conferred a practical advantage, that person's superior performance should prove it beyond doubt. There would no longer be two distinct groups within the organization: one under constant scrutiny for displays of brilliance and the other assumed to have limited potential. Today, little evidence is required to confirm the genius expected of those with prominent credentials, while the brilliant work of those outside this group is largely ignored or passed off as a fluke. The result of having no record of past educational achievement would be that current learning and performance, and not past history, would set the standards for acceptable achievement. In theory, of course, this is how our system is supposed to work, but, in actual practice in most large organizations, it doesn't work that way, and everyone knows it.

After much data collection and research about education and performance Ivar Berg wrote, "The search for evidence to give weight to economic arguments supporting the use of educational credentials for jobs has not been conspicuously successful."[2] Berg reported the results of United States Air Force research in his book *Education and Jobs,* with the conclusion that,

Years of education are:
a. only moderately related to objective measures of aptitude;
b. a poor predictor of success in training;

c. almost unrelated to objective measures of proficiency on the
   job.
In summing up his study, Berg observed there are:

> . . .grounds for doubting that it is useful to regard education in
> America within a simplified framework in which a person's
> *years of schooling* are taken as a significant measure; schools
> are too diverse and people too differentiated to permit the rou-
> tine and automatic confusion of the morals, motives, and capa-
> bilities of the licensed with their licenses. The experience with
> marriages in Western society may illustrate this point.

Still, we persist in using evidence of past educational achievement as the major qualifier in the workplace, while denying the
reality of competence in day-to-day life experience.

Competence

The mind of the student who is pushed or compelled to trudge
through school in order to qualify is not unlike film haphazardly
exposed in a camera: pictures are taken without regard to the aes-
thetics or composition of the setting. A society in which schooling
is used as proof of competence misses the point because it relies
not on the quality of its photographs, but upon the amount of film
exposed. How incredulous that we will not accept beautifully developed finished prints as demonstrated competence but will insist
on finding testimony that all the frames on the film have been
filled. In other words, where competence is concerned, we often
ignore the evidence in order to look for clues. Millions of American
workers face this standard as a daily review of their performance,
simply because the organizations in which they work have not seen
beyond this ridiculousness. In effect, the boss is saying, "I don't
care what you can do, I want to know what you've done. And what
have you done that will get me off the hook if I demonstrate open
confidence in you and you fail?"

Personality theories tell us that we are fundamentally similar,
but widely different in skills, talents, and natural abilities. So what
does it mean to be competent? Ask ten different people what it
means to be competent and you might get ten dramatically different answers. My definition for the purposes of this book is this: a
competent person is one who is able to perform a job or task with
sufficient skill to be seen by both the recipient (customer or bene-
ficiary) and the provider (one's boss) of the service or function as
having performed it successfully. Obviously this definition leaves a
lot of room for subjective opinion, because the recipient of the
service and the provider may have different standards or different

expectations. We have to apply a "reasonable person" approach, as is used in common law, to make this definition workable.

Artists, writers, athletes, and entrepreneurs have the ability to offer their work in such a manner that it can stand alone on its own merits. Millions of others, however, are engaged in a vast range of occupations where a lack of certain credentials precludes opportunities to demonstrate their potential. For example, movie actor Al Pacino failed all of his high school subjects except English, but a screen test is ample proof of the quality of his work. Likewise, television news anchorman Peter Jennings dropped out of high school in the tenth grade, but his news delivery and demeanor on the evening news are proof of his competence. I would venture to say a potential Al Pacino or Peter Jennings can be found in most any company in most any industry. Some of these people spend years doing excellent jobs, but are never considered for promotion because they lack credentials unrelated to their current job or the job they would get if promoted. Others, whose superior work performance is easy to observe, are simply recognized as belonging to a category all by themselves.

In the arts, sports, and music industries, those who hire and promote talent sometimes have their bad decisions come back to haunt them. For example, imagine being the person who told Elvis Presley he would never make it in the music business, or one of the 121 publishers who rejected Robert M. Pirsig's book, *Zen and the Art of Motorcycle Maintenance,* which became a bestseller in 1974 and is still in print. Given spotlight attention, genuine competence has a way of showing itself, regardless of whether or not everyone recognizes it. But, in the everyday workplace, we seldom have the benefit of this type of feedback. No one keeps track of the people who were not hired because they seemed to lack ambition, didn't say the right thing during a job interview, or misspelled a word on their resume. We don't know how many of them go on to demonstrate that it was a mistake not to hire them. The result is that, even with a poor track record of hiring decisions and no means of collecting data for course correction, we continue to act as if we're making good decisions. Thus, those whose job it is to hire new employees can spend a lifetime career interviewing and hiring thousands of employees, while continuing to make the same kind of errors in judgment that they made during their first week on the job. Moreover, the human psyche has a way of remembering better the data that confirm opinions and beliefs already held. [3] So, in effect when an employer chooses not to hire someone because of an unconscious personal bias, very little evidence will be needed to reinforce this opinion, but overwhelming evidence (which is unavailable) will be needed to effect a change of mind.

If we are continually restrained by not getting a chance to demonstrate our competence, we have a difficult time gaining a sense of our own authority. We have a tendency to be unsure of ourselves just enough to defer to others, even in areas where we have experience and expertise but not enough confidence to offer our views authoritatively. When we pay too much attention to what "experts" say without critical inquiry, in effect we deny our own experience and discount our own intelligence.

The Intelligence Myths

The myths about the phenomenon we call intelligence are legendary. Some people think intelligence can be measured by an IQ test; others argue that we have multiple intelligences. What I want to do here is to clear up any myth about what can be expected of the ordinary person, whom we would consider to possess average intelligence. The notion that occupations categorized as "professional" require above-average intelligence is simply not true. People with average and below "intelligence" test scores can, and do, become doctors, lawyers, engineers, accountants, and a myriad of other types of occupations considered professional. Indeed, the greatest range in intelligence as measured by IQ is found, not among those in lower-level jobs, but rather among "professionals."[4]

Expertise: The Mystery of Mastery

How do you define expertise? My definition of a person with expertise (an expert) is someone who knows a particular specialty so thoroughly that reliance on rules and procedures in proving a point or reaching a conclusion is unnecessary. Experts rely on visceral, gut responses, and, because of their advanced knowledge (based on assimilation of theory and experience), they are nearly always correct.

There are two short-cuts to creating the appearance of being an expert. The first is to make a religion of skepticism. A person who doubts everything can feign expertise by never taking a stand. Moreover, it is easy to make another person look foolish by asking questions about matters known only to the questioner, even if the questions are irrelevant. Some critics argue that Socrates was this kind an expert, although he openly professed his own ignorance. We have only Plato's written word as evidence to the contrary.

The second quick claim to expertise is made by the believer who puts total faith in one authority, such as religious doctrine. Arguing that one source provides all of the answers needed leads one to use authority as a substitute for expertise and to bypass reason in favor of recall. Such an expert is not required to think, but only to remember a passage of text for every occasion.

One has to study the concept of expertise itself to realize just how little we really know. Every major criminal trial demonstrates this without question, as witness after witness presents testimony diametrically opposed to that of the other "experts." Many of the subjects taught in school survive revolutions which, in time, reveal past experts to have been nothing but imposters.

The awarding of doctorate degrees is supposed to occur as a result of demonstrable additions to humanity's growing body of knowledge, and many are awarded for this very reason. Still, if you've developed a habit of naturally deferring to people with Ph.D's, go to any university and look at a listing of their doctoral dissertations. Chances are, you'll feel bamboozled. I have known people with graduate degrees who are too embarrassed to say what their doctoral study was about, yet they won't hesitate to let others know the value of their own opinions. Several years ago, I pleaded with a seminar leader to tell me what her dissertation was about, simply because I was very interested in the subject of management psychology which she was teaching. She never would tell me exactly, except to say that it had something to do with accounting and mass transit and was really only an exercise of going through the motions.

My point is that jumping through hoops has little to do with discovery or with adding substance to the frontiers knowledge. But it has a lot to do with power and the abuse of power. Going through the motions amounts to paying tribute to a hierarchical organization by paying the fees, dotting the i's and crossing the t's. You affirm their power to grant status, and they reciprocate by giving you a title which confers rank. In short, claims of esoteric knowledge and expertise often represent little more than a pose. And it's easy to keep up such a pose precisely because there is a strong desire among the general public to believe that those in positions of power and authority really know what they are talking about.

Fortunately, my own experience with people with graduate degrees has been mostly positive. Many of my friends with doctorate degrees are among the most intellectually stimulating people I have ever met. Having taken complete responsibility for their own education, they are, without exception, unpretentious about their credentials. Those who really seek knowledge realize just how little they know and, further, how little is known. Unfortunately, I am also acquainted with the other type of Ph.D.—those preoccupied not with intellectual inquiry, but with their own status and hierarchical standing. The bottom line is: beware of experts who profess to have the truth nailed down! Carry a claw-hammer at all times.

Should anything I've said up to this point lead you to believe that I am in any way anti-intellectual, then, I am in serious error. Nothing could further from the truth. I believe the life of the mind, as I'm sure most sincere academics will acknowledge, is one of the greatest joys of living. It's the behavior of people who use academic credentials as evidence of something that they do not posses that I detest.

It is indeed a paradox that expectations about formal education lead to unrealistic convictions about its results. You'd think a person would remember more from college experience than from earlier years of schooling, but, according to professors Stephen A. Stumpf and Joel R. DeLuca, authors of *Learning to Use What You Already Know,* the reverse is true:

> Learning is often cumulative; we would not be able to read the secondary school texts if we did not learn how to read and develop a strong vocabulary in primary school. Nor would college calculus be accessible if algebra was not learned in high school.

This is why going through the motions is so injurious to the birth of knowledge. If people obtain credentials without genuine interest in their subjects, they will not remember what everyone else assumes they already know. Moreover, to defend themselves, those who mask their ignorance with a pose of expertise cannot resort to reason, but must try to discredit those who question their judgment.

Interest and Enthusiasm

In a system of higher education where so many attend for the sake of qualification, where major subjects are often chosen with little prior practical knowledge of the field to be studied, shouldn't a person's current level of interest in the field count as much or more than length of exposure to the subject? Aren't a burning desire, born of genuine interest, and a vision of what one intends to accomplish more important than a familiarity based on a foggy history?

In the presidential election of 1980, candidate Ronald Regan was accused of being unqualified to be U.S. president. He was, after all, an actor by profession, even though he had been governor of California. Today most Republicans would argue that Ronald Regan was a far better president than George Bush, who had the perfect resume to be president. In the 1988 election, when George Bush ran against Michael Dukakis, he was touted as the most qualified person to ever seek the office of president of the United

States. But history will not likely be so kind to George Bush. Although he may have been qualified in the sense of our current credentialing system, he lacked the "vision thing." George Bush may have been "qualified" to be president, but a significant number of the people who voted him into office voted him out in 1992.

An associate of mine once told me about a young woman he had dated who had a degree in French literature, but who didn't know what a metaphor was and who had never heard of Jean Paul Sartre. Now, I can understand how a person might have a degree in French literature without knowing what a metaphor is or be unaware of Sartre's contribution to French philosophy, but I don't how anyone could be genuinely interested in French literature without knowing these things.

Qualified, But Not Suited

Being qualified has nothing to do with suitability—nothing. So, how unfortunate it is that, if we can get the right credential, produce the right resume, and find the proper coaching in order to say the right things in an interview, we can be assured of getting a job that we absolutely shouldn't have. People in jobs for which they are qualified but not well suited set the standard for mediocre performance. A consequence of a qualification system that makes horizontal and vertical job movement difficult is that a person who becomes qualified for a particular line of work becomes trapped in a sense. Millions of people perform jobs grudgingly because they have "paid their dues" to get qualified. They will readily admit they'd be happier doing some other type of work, if only it were not so hard to qualify and if only it paid more.

To appreciate the tragic waste in money and effort that results, we have to realize that asking who is *qualified* is the wrong question. We need to ask who is *competent* and allow them to offer proof through demonstration of their skills. This may sound like a cumbersome system to put into practice, but it couldn't possibly be less efficient than the methods we currently use to achieve qualification. Millions of students invest years of study in disciplines, the actual practice of which conflicts with their natural abilities. Every organization of people engaged in diverse activities will, with a little investigation, prove this point beyond question. Colleges and universities send legions of square pegs to fit round holes, and round pegs to fit square ones, because they pay too much attention to the *class* and not enough to the *student*. When we use the word "entitlement," we most often refer to social or economic programs, such as welfare or aid to dependent children. Our educational system, however, promotes another entitlement phenomenon which is seldom acknowledged and rarely, if ever, discussed. It's not the sense of entitlement that one gets from working toward a degree with the expectation of finding complementary employment. No, the sort of entitlement I'm referring to is the kind which compels some people with credentials to assume and act as if they are over-qualified for whatever it is they are asked to do and to never perform at an acceptable level because of it.

If you've been in the workplace a long time, you probably know what I'm talking about. Take, for example, the engineer who spent years in advanced engineering courses, not out of interest or desire to do a better job, but specifically because they would look good on a resume. The quality of his resume was his principle preoccupation. He often boasted that he was rapidly reaching a level of qualification so impressive he could not possibly be turned down for any position by any company in his field. He was so qualified, in fact, he almost never encountered a situation worthy of his exceptional skills. He rarely did any work and was eventually fired, but I'm sure he found another job quickly. He had a great resume.

Now, one could argue that someone who fails to perform on the job presents a behavioral problem clearly differentiated from an issue about credentials and qualification. I agree. But I have never heard the problem of *credentialed entitlement* openly acknowledged or discused, even though it is ubiquitous in nature.

Perhaps the phenomenon of entitlement is more easily observable from a different viewpoint. For example, there are many jobs which people perform as an interim measure while they work their way through school or until they can find a better job. The occupation of waiter and waitress is a case in point. Who has not been served in restaurants by those who clearly act as if waiting on tables is beneath their station in life? The puzzle is, the only way they could prove that waiting on tables is below their abilities would be to do it so well that their superiority over the job became self-evident. Who has not been impressed by the waiter or waitress who masters his or her job to perfection—a job which most people believe is simple but few are able to perform satisfactorily? Poor food service is so common that good service stands out. Unfortunately, the assumption of entitlement based solely upon one's educational credentials seems very nearly as prevalent as inferior service in a restaurant.

One of the greatest paradoxes of American culture is that we adamantly profess to be a classless society, and yet we are quite possibly the most class conscious society on the face of the earth. If such were not the case, who among us waited on tables would be of little consequence.

Benjamin DeMott once wrote, "The will to believe the mythology of classlessness is rooted in personal narrative: the stories of our self-mythologizing lives." As an illustration, he offered the following vignette:

> Once upon a time, says the voice of memory, I lived through a situation in which rank order was based on ability, work held the key to privilege, all possessed the right to earn privilege, and the allocation of rewards was disinterested and just. I and others stood equal at the starting line in this situation, dependent solely on personal resources. I was free to race with the pacemakers or hang back and finish last. I knew the contest was consequential for life fortunes. I knew that doing better or worse was up to me. I knew that in this situation—the place and time wherein I individually determined my fate and fashioned my unique self—fairness ruled.[5]

And when our long-time friends recall these experiences to us we say: right, we were there, remember? For some, such a narrative may be true, but most of us who have reached middle-age or later are aware of the self-serving nature of human beings. Whether we want to admit it or not, we are conscious that the ethos of winning in a competitive society makes its members acutely aware of class. Thus, we are not surprised that people judge us by our occupation, our dress, our speech, our possessions, and as many other distinguishing characteristics as they can detect. Clearly, the notion of suitability can be very subjective.

Suited, But Not Qualified

Every now and then someone with totally fraudulent credentials pops up and grabs the spotlight of public attention, someone who has been performing a job as a "professional" with counterfeit credentials. A seldom noticed but amazing thing about these occurrences is that a significant number of the people who are discovered to be without credentials have been doing a good job. Poor performance is seldom the reason they're discovered to be imposters. Now, I'm not recommending we resort to dishonest methods of qualification, but isn't it strange that people with natural talent and aptitude can perform well enough to be accepted as professionals while incompetents with credentials cannot be stopped from practice, even when their incompetence is clearly obvious to everyone?

Albert Einstein was well suited to physics, Thomas Edison to innovation, Abraham Lincoln to law, Charles Darwin to natural science, and George Benard Shaw to the arts. Today, given their educational backgrounds, these individuals would not be "qualified" even to comment about these subjects. This is not progress.

Qualified and Suited

It's not surprising that the history of both Eastern and Western culture has long recognized the need to match the tasks required of people with their natural talents. Plato wrote about it in *The Republic,* and the concept of Right Livelihood has for centuries been a fundamental tenet of Buddhism. People who are well-suited to their jobs provide the model of performance to which the rest aspire. In her book *Do What You Love the Money Will Follow,* Marsha Sinetar writes,

> The very best way to relate to our work is to choose it. Right Livelihood is predicated upon conscious choice. Unfortunately, since we learn early to act on what others say, value, and expect, we often find ourselves a long way down the wrong road before realizing we did not actually choose our work....Work is a natural vehicle for self-expression because we spend most of our time in its thrall. It simply makes sense not to turn off our personality, squelch our real abilities, forget our need for stimulation and personal growth forty hours out of every week.

The notion of choosing your work in an ailing economy may seem selfish or unrealistic, especially if there are not enough jobs to go around, but this idea of choosing work, of Right Livelihood, is a long-term posture. If you expect work should be fulfilling, such a stance is necessary to avoid perpetually running out of steam and enthusiasm. There is absolutely nothing wrong with believing that work is not an end in itself, but rather a means to economic sustenance. Still, even when that's the reason for working, choosing work in accordance with your natural affinities makes the most sense.

Motivation and the Big Misunderstanding

From a psychological perspective, motivation can be a complex subject, but in everyday practice it boils down to enthusiasm. In the current lingo, we call it attitude. The magnitude of the problems associated with attitude becomes immediately clear when we consider the person who is qualified to perform a particular job, but who has no enthusiasm for it. There may be many reasons for the lack of eagerness—the job may not pay enough, it may be boring, it may not represent much of a challenge, management may be unreasonable. The reason doesn't matter nearly so much as the cloud of confusion a lack of enthusiasm brings to the subject of qualification.

For several years an associate of mine, who was a warehouse foreman, hired entry-level personnel based upon his own personal observations of them in other job settings. He was always on the look-out for people who were doing their jobs with enthusiasm and evidence of mastery. Busboys, grocery store personnel, gas pump attendants—the nature of their work was irrelevant. What counted was their visible enthusiasm. The foreman would give these individuals a card and say, "If you ever need a job look me up." His method worked very well. The people he hired as a result of these encounters often had little experience in warehousing, they were not always "qualified," but they brought their enthusiasm with them. When they put it to work, no one complained about their qualifications, even though some of the jobs were technically complex.

People who perform their jobs without at least some degree of enthusiasm "appear" not to be qualified, regardless of their credentials. The result is that this perception is likely to degrade or undermine confidence in the whole qualification system. Poor performance because of a bad attitude, for whatever reason, is a management problem, but not everyone will perceive it as such. Some people, especially those who feel they are better qualified, will view a credential holder's lack of enthusiasm as being proof that the wrong person has the job. This perception may or may not be true, but it is very important to employee morale that the qualification process both for hiring and for promotions is thought to be and is, in fact, fair.

For more than a decade I have actively studied the subject of motivation, and I've discovered a great secret: the reason thousands of books and tapes by assorted motivational gurus are gathering dust in people's closets is that *purpose inspires method*, period. When you have purpose, relevance pops out everywhere. The motivational industry has developed technique for making sales, but it does not sell purpose because no one has yet figured out how to provide it to someone else.

Purpose can't be given to us. It is something we must discover for ourselves. Purpose is sort of the Holy Grail of one's life. As much as you may be temporarily inspired by motivational books and tapes, finding purpose is a personal enterprise which cannot be bought. "Desire, deep desire, is the sap of the tree of life."[6] It has become cliche to say that "knowledge is power," but the seldom noticed secondary effect is that knowledge is the shaper of purpose. In other words, knowledge gives life to purpose. Many of the motivation industry's techniques may be effective, but, for the person without a powerful sense of sustained purpose, the desire to make use of them sort of fizzles out.

In the movie *City Slickers,* Jack Palance plays a rugged trail boss who raises one finger to make his point: the secret of life is one thing, but *you* have to figure out what it is. Good advice. I might go one step further and add that one path to finding purpose exists in striving to move beyond the external trappings of society. What society itself dictates as being important counts very little when compared to what you really think all by yourself. Author of *Zen and the Art of Making a Living,* Laurence G. Boldt, writes,

> Your life's work does not exist "out there," in a world apart. You can't order up the perfect career or set of careers the way you might order a lawn mower from the Sears catalogue. Being too concerned with what is "out there" before you know what you want "in here" puts you in a position of powerlessness.

Powerlessness, indeed. There is no more haunting feeling than to become turbo-charged at a motivational pep rally and then to run out of enthusiasm for no apparent reason. A strong sense of purpose is the only sure way to avoid feeling powerless.

Communication: The Universal Credential

Regardless of whether our dominant strengths are mathematical, mechanical, creative, artistic, interpersonal, or highly technical, there is one credential we carry with us at all times: our ability to communicate. Nothing projects our level of competence with greater certainty than the way we write and speak—especially the latter. To be seen as eminently "promotable," you must be considered capable of communicating at any level within an organization, without appearing to talk up or down to individuals on that level. The single greatest common denominator of successful people is a large vocabulary, and yet few people who strive to climb the organizational ladder seem to appreciate the importance of being able to communicate well. Even college students, who seek out courses of every conceivable description for the sake of career advancement, typically avoid basic courses in language and communication if they're not required.

In 1988, the Associated Press ran a story about a California teacher who had graduated from college with a degree in education and had taught for 18 years, but could not read. Imagine being articulate enough to hide such a fact for more than two decades. Harder to imagine still is that a degree in teaching does not ensure that the holder of the degree can read.

It is a common assumption to believe that we are stuck with the way we talk and that there is little we can do to change it. But the movies are a constant reminder to the contrary. Actors and actresses from different countries repeatedly demonstrate that it is possible to change one's speaking style convincingly and even change one's accent. Clear writing and clear speaking are the result of clear thinking. It should come as no surprise, then, that a person will not be "promotable" if judged to be thinking poorly. Every time we speak out loud or write a memo, we call attention to the quality of our thinking. If unclear communication is a result of unclear thinking, the remedy is easy—unless of course, thinking seems too hard.

Command of subject matter is judged through the way it is communicated, regardless of the nature or level of expertise of the communicator. Former President George Bush spoke in incomplete sentences and avoided pronouns like they were broccoli, and he failed to be reelected. On the other hand, commentators like Connie Chung, Phil Donahue, Bonnie Erbe, Gary Fife, John Hockinberry, Ted Kopple, David McCullough, Cokie Roberts, Roger Rosenblatt, Richard Rodriquez, Bernard Shaw, Carol Simpson, and Ray Suarez can bring the appearance of credibility to practically any subject through their articulate delivery.

Communication style is sometimes learned through socialization at colleges and universities outside the formal classroom. It's easier to talk to people who are familiar with the same books, the same dress code, the same interests in art and literature, and the same kinds of music as your own. Socialization, which relies on reciprocal communication, is very important to being seen by others as qualified for any task. It may be, then, that the greatest qualifying advantage to be gained from college attendance is a greater ability to communicate—which is no small prize.

People who learn to write well do so, in large part, by reading. People who learn to speak well do so by talking. The passive nature of traditional education is one of the greatest tragedies of the system. To have students attend classes year after year and still be unable to clearly articulate what is on their minds is an absurdity I find incomprehensible. Impromptu camera interviews with Americans air daily on local television stations throughout the nation, revealing a citizenry which might well be intelligent, but whose inability to speak articulately is pitiful. Little wonder there is so much violence and conflict in America, when millions of supposedly educated people cannot communicate above a fifth-grade level with their neighbors. It has recently occurred to me that my own thrust toward self-education was due in part to a sense of frustration over my personal ability to communicate.

So, if you have similar problems communicating, I have great news: books and conversation are very inexpensive. Your posture and commitment to lifelong learning may have a greater bearing on your future success than anything you learn from this book. Indeed, strong interests propel us toward discovery, which is the surest way to build competence and expertise. And there is no better way to increase our powers of communication than to have something exciting to write and talk about. As you'll see in the following chapter, a good place to begin this kind of inquiry in earnest is in the development of self-knowledge.

Chapter Six

Leverage, Options, and Choices

A professionalized society is more like blackjack, and getting a degree is like being dealt nineteen. You could try for more, but why?

—James Fallows

Self-Knowledge: The Greatest Career Leverage You Have

S elf-knowledge may seem out of place with respect to proving you are qualified, but it is a central issue in the process and ethos of qualification. Abraham Maslow has cautioned us that if we deliberately set out to accomplish less than we are capable of we will be unhappy for the rest of our lives. But the only way to be truly deliberate is to understand yourself. We have no greater leverage over our own lives than through the development of self-knowledge. The power of knowing oneself and one's potential is available only to those who pay attention to the subtle aspects of life. Those who do not pay attention confuse the map with the territory.

We recognize those who know the difference as "people who know where they are going." We acknowledge their sense of purpose by getting out of their way; we help to clear obstacles from their path; we assist them without question, as if we know intuitively that helping them do what they seem bent on doing is the right thing to do. Moreover, we do this for others regardless of whether they are friends, family, co-workers, subordinates or bosses. Purpose promotes its own momentum, gains its own velocity, creating a force that not only enables cooperation but also encourages aid. You have only to think of the enthusiasm and support

93

we have for the Olympic athlete to understand how this contagious phenomenon works in practice.

The greatest access we have to developing purpose is through self-understanding, and the principal requisite to self-understanding is to better understand others. Fortunately, this is an enterprise you are never too old to start. In fact, it may be easier to accomplish the more experience you have at living.

Understanding Human Behavior

Think for a moment about how many times you used mathematics last week. How about English? Upon reflection, the answers will probably surprise you especially with the latter—we do very little without the use of language. How much did you do last week that involved human beings and interpersonal relations? Now, contrast these three fields of study with your formal education. How much time did you spend studying math and English? How much time did you spend studying human behavior?

This little exercise makes it painfully obvious that we have largely ignored one of the subjects that is most important to us. Not much happens without some type of human interaction. Not that we don't learn a great deal about human behavior as we grow up. We do. We develop what might be called an intuitive feel for understanding ourselves and other people, but since we don't study it in a formal, comparative sense, we don't have a conscious awareness of that understanding, which puts us at a severe disadvantage. We're forced to feel our way through situations without the added benefit of rational analysis. Moreover, once we make a few significant errors in the process of feeling our way through difficult human relations, we begin to dread the whole process and start avoiding important matters or leaving them to experts.

To be sure, the study of human behavior is a subjective enterprise. All we will ever be able to do is speculate about many areas and use our best judgment. But an educated, reasoned effort, combined with intuition, can bring us much closer to a sense of reality in our human relationships than either method can by itself. The process is circular: learning about human behavior means learning about oneself, which means learning about others.

It's worth a great deal to us simply to know there are other people who are a lot like us. Growing up, we're taught that we are unique individuals. Yes, we are, but we also develop personalities that are similar to those of others. These personalities, which might also be characterized as defense postures or ways of coping or adapting to the world, contain an extraordinary amount of information about how we might best discover and use our unique talents. Adequate self-knowledge can save us years of effort and thousands of dollars pursuing credentials in subject areas that seem interesting and attractive but fly in the face of our individual, inborn talents.

Personality Theory

Personality theories demonstrate that when we compare large numbers of people, they exhibit different preferences in relating to the world. These preferences take shape as skills, talents, interests, and natural affinities. Further, they provide a frame or a posture that makes a person's particular life-stance recognizable when we know what to look for. Two of the most popular measures of personality are the Myers-Briggs profile and the Enneagram model. The sheer amount of data accompanying the Myers-Briggs is valuable for making comparisons. The Enneagram is an excellent tool for discovering insight into motivation.

Beyond these, the best model I have found for discovering one's strength, and subsequently relating that strength to the workplace, is Ned Herrman's Whole-Brain Theory. It is equally useful for self-understanding and for gaining perspective on today's society. As set forth in his book, *The Creative Brain*, Herrman's model puts shape to a great deal of what we have learned from experience but have never been able to characterize and categorize. Consciously recognizing what we had been only vaguely aware of before helps us transfer intuition into knowledge, and this produces confidence. The whole-brain model also allows us to recognize the value of human differences—a subject which, when better understood, makes life's journey easier, more enjoyable, and less frustrating.

Taking the left-brain right-brain concept a bit further, Herrman uses the terms upper and lower to divide the left and right hemispheres of the brain into four-quadrants. For testing purposes he uses the letters A, B, C, and D as a reference for each quadrant. The four distinct areas represent four ways of thinking:

- A– upper left: analytical, logical, critical, and mathematical.
- B– lower left: procedural sequential, technical, controlled, and detailed.
- C– lower right: emotional, symbolic, spiritual, and interpersonal.
- D– upper right: spatial, holistic, intuitive, innovative, and metaphoric.

These four thinking modes amount to perceptions of value (my term) rather than physiological certainties. The brain is a highly integrative organ. To say that a given way of knowing or thinking occurs only in one hemisphere is overly simplistic. Nevertheless, it is extremely useful to apprehend that these ways of knowing are really core human values and that, as individuals, we rate them in a hierarchical order.

It is not my intention to delve too far into personality theory, but to point out these models for your own further study. The Recommended Reading section at the back of this book lists additional titles concerning these subjects. I can't emphasize strongly enough the value of such an endeavor. Self-knowledge is as fundamental to career development as water is to plant growth.

Capitalizing on Strengths

Most people develop some sense of their natural talents and abilities as they mature. The talent and special skills of athletes, musicians, and math wizards seem obvious because they are so pronounced. Some of us gain more insight about our strengths by being far more conscious of what we dislike than by what we are drawn toward. Indeed, for some of us, using the process of elimination to categorize what we don't want to do may be the best avenue for discovering what we would really like to do.

One of the difficulties in discovering your strengths stems from the fact that our society values some strengths more than others. If we grow up unaware that differences are natural, normal, and even desirable, the result is that we see only the societally recognized strengths; everything else is viewed as weakness. For generations our culture has placed great importance on the left-brain skills of logic and analysis, with particular emphasis on rules, order, and specialization. It is only in recent years that we have awakened to the realization that these skills must be balanced with creativity and innovation, and that people-relating skills have a foundational role in the health and nurturing of the human psyche. These latter attributes are critical to the workplace, and the fact that we have largely ignored their importance for so long is easily provable by examining our multibillion dollar stress industry.

Our perception of our individual strengths forms the backbone of the life-stance we adopt. Many people view their priorities at work in terms of their own strengths. This is evident in organizations where people change jobs often. As individuals move into new positions, they then try to shift management's attention to their own special way of doing things.

For those of us who grew up with little sense of our strengths, determining what we are best at is likely to have been largely a hit or miss proposition. And, if you have made some incompatible career choices along the way, your self-image is likely to have suffered. If you're like me, you may have grown up thinking you should be good at everything and, therefore, assume something's wrong with you if you're not. What a relief to discover that differences are normal—natural preferences that enable us to excel far better than if our talents were equally distributed. It's no longer threatening to think of ourselves as being in some way handicapped, as Richard Bolles explains:

> *Every* job-hunter is handicapped. The only question is: what is the handicap, and how much does it show?...There are, let us say, 13,000 truly different skills that human beings possess. You, as an average job-hunter, have only 700 of these. Believe me, you're handicapped. Sit down and put Mozart on your stereo or CD player, when you're searching for some humility.[1]

In Western culture, we have never become comfortable with our differences to the degree that we naturally understand them as advantages. Katherine Benziger and Anne Sohn's thesis in *The Art Of Using Your Whole Brain* is that once you know your strengths objectively, you can become even better at them with less effort than is required to work on an area of weakness. In other words, it is easier to go from good to excellent than from poor to good. Once excellence is achieved, you are able to work on a weakness from a position of confidence; self-esteem is not in jeopardy.

Posture

In the early '70s Robert J. Ringer wrote a bestseller entitled *Looking Out For Number One*. Social critics claimed it was evidence that we had reached a point of moral bankruptcy. Although Ringer's assertions may have been distasteful, he was socially astute in demonstrating that "posture" and dealing from positions of strength are of extreme importance in day-to-day experience. Posture is similar to reputation in that it is the status, state, or social level which you *appear* to have reached. It can also have negative connotations. You may have assumed a posture much less representative of your abilities than is actually the case.

Posture may be thought of as a derivative or an expression of self-esteem: how others see us determines how we see ourselves. Posture conveys expectations in the way we are to be treated or in the way we will be rewarded. For example, if I have achieved a reputation as an expert financial advisor, a client will expect to reward me well for my advice, but the client who takes me for a beginner might not feel I am worthy of a commission, even if my advice brings in a great deal of money. The good fortune will be attributed to luck rather than my skill, and a reward for my services will not seem deserved. Posture in this context would be my acting from a stance of competence regardless of whether or not I have established a reputation based on competence.

A meritorious posture is the natural product of a commitment to personal mastery. It may be based in part upon bluff, but, to be successful in the long run, it must be based upon genuine competence.

Labels

The primary way we keep track of effort in a meritocracy is through the use of labels. We use terms, such as B.A., M.A., and Ph.D, to identify educational levels, and names like master bricklayer and journeyman carpenter to represent competence and experience in various occupations. Labels can limit or liberate. People who accept the label of dropout often behave like one. As motivational gurus have always said, "Think poor and you will be poor."

Labels have the capacity to psychologically cripple as well as to empower. Understand this paradox, and you will possess a secret of success that surprisingly few ever realize. Studies confirm, people are so influenced by labels that a simple change in job title from supervisor to assistant can be enough to inhibit their performance.[2]

Clearly, we should not use labels as a means of stereotyping groups or individuals. But merely to say that is inadequate. Inherent in our use of language is a tremendous tendency to limit by tagging and labeling everything we come into contact with. Simply to warn against labeling is to deny how persistent we are at it. Labels and stereotypes are like sparks in a dry forest. It seems impossible to stamp them out, precisely because labels themselves become templates that form the structure of paradigms or our way of seeing things. In other words, labels without reflection constitute mental models that we use without thinking.

Something deeply embedded in the human psyche's compulsion to limit awareness by simplifying experience dovetails with the ethos of capitalism to foster prejudice. In his book *Being and Nothingness*, French philosopher Jean Paul Sartre described this notion by suggesting that the obligation of tradespeople is to restrain their actions to that of predictable performance. Sartre wrote,

> Their condition is wholly one of ceremony. The public demands of them that they realize it as a ceremony; there is the dance of the grocer, of the tailor, of the auctioneer, by which they endeavor to persuade their clientele that they are nothing but a grocer, an auctioneer, a tailor. A grocer who dreams is offensive to the buyer, because such a grocer is not wholly a grocer.

The old saying "birds of a feather flock together" is a good way to demonstrate the importance of understanding labeling. When we use broad labels to categorize people in groups, such as middle class, lower class, street people, homeless, rich, poor, dropout, or college graduate, we cannot help but set mental limits within which we expect people in these categories to behave. We do the same thing with respect to ourselves and our associates. Without purposeful awareness it becomes hard to see ourselves differently from the people with whom we regularly spend a lot of time. The wisdom to be drawn from this experience is simple: Seek people out who want what you want, or who have already achieved what you hope to achieve.

Cultural expectations implicit in labels act as barriers for vertical advancement in society through subtle ways of letting people know they are "off-sides" or "out of bounds." Plato divided the work to be accomplished within a given society by assigning three social classes: rulers, auxiliaries, and craftsmen. Such cultural expectations generally prescribe who is to do what.

Occupations are influenced by the hierarchical structure of society and the labels that accompany each gradation. For example, one model suggests that each level of society has its own attitudes about work, complete with prescriptions for which work which people should do. The major hurdle here for the individual is to break the crust of expectations imposed by others and learn to follow one's own lead. The pressure involved in this pursuit is so great that many people—even if they are miserable—will not make a serious change in their work lives, without the express approval of others who are not in a position to judge the situation objectively.

These problems have been with us for generations. Near the middle of the nineteenth century, Henry David Thoreau wrote:

> I see young men, my townsmen, whose misfortune it is to have inherited farms, houses, barns, cattle, and farming tools; for these are more easily acquired than got rid of. Better if they had been born in the open pasture and suckled by a wolf, that they might have seen with clearer eyes what field they were called to labor in.[3]

Strategies for proving you are qualified require persistent awareness of how vulnerable we are to limited thinking and how our economic system works to disunite us from others. Family and friends warn us about taking risks, seeing us as limited by the labels of our current occupation. If we try and fail, they will say, "I told you so." If we try and succeed, they will say, "We knew you could do it all along," forgetting that they warned us against it initially. In order to change the hierarchical structure of society, it is first necessary to change the hierarchical notions in the heads of the participants.

Experience

How often have you heard the saying, "Want some experience? Get a job. Want a job? Get some experience." This problem is obviously more difficult for people who are starting out in life than for those who have spent many years in the workplace, although it can be a problem for both. If you don't have the experience, then you must use your educational credentials or your natural abilities and aptitudes to gain opportunities for getting experience. If you have the experience, then you must use evidence based on your experience to prove you should have the opportunity to get the job. Experience can be documented and presented in a way that can be more convincing than paper certificates or diplomas from institutions, no matter how prestigious. The section on portfolio development later in this chapter explains how to document your experience.

For all of the criticism we shower on the federal government, the civil service does a creditable job in recognizing the value of experience. Its promotional policies give far more weight to experience than to educational achievement.[4] Yes, education can often be substituted for experience in federal jobs, just as the reverse can be true, but the weight given to actual experience is what counts. The down side is that civil service policies do not give much weight to actual performance when compared to seniority. It is certainly ironic, but not well known, that the federal bureaucracy is actually less bureaucratic with regard to personnel promotions than is private industry.[5] This paradox is due in part to what I referred to earlier as the *willingness factor*. You can see how there would be more autonomy for managers in a bureaucracy than in a private organization. There is more job security. Thus, there is less risk involved in promoting subordinates: The measure is always assumed to be "safe."[6]

There is another aspect worth considering in trying to determine why a bureaucracy would act more reasonably in regard to actual experience over credentials. The true effects of bureaucracy may be misunderstood. In *Education and Jobs*, Ivar Berg writes,

> The irony will not be lost on some that the nonrational use of formal credentials, which might be taken as a significant symptom of "bureaupathology," is more likely to be found in our great private enterprises than in our governmental apparatus. The capacity of industry leaders to temper the effect of the marketplace in an age of subsidies, tax shelters, stockpiling programs, depreciation allowances, and rulings that facilitate the deduction of fines and damages for price conspiracies as "ordi-

nary business expenses" is undoubtedly related to the luxurious consumption of high-priced labor. As a consequence, it is the public that shops in the competitive market so favored in economists' models. It is the public's hired manager who must act the role of the entrepreneur in imaginatively combining scarce human resources.

Perhaps, as we aspire to reinvent government, we might also rethink private enterprise and the utilization of skills by employees who could demonstrate them convincingly, if only they had the opportunity to do so.

Skills

There are a number of ways to approach the subject of skills, but for our purposes they all boil down to one idea: to enhance our marketability in the workplace we must know our strengths, not only intuitively but also objectively. It is not enough to have only an intuitive or vague sense of our strengths. Many skills are transferable. We take these skills with us wherever we go, so it is vital that we be able to enumerate to anyone who is interested precisely what those skills are. Two books offer excellent methodologies for assessing skills and placing them in an insightful hierarchy: *What Color is Your Parachute?* by Richard Nelson Bolles and *Zen and the Art of Making a Living*, by Laurence G. Boldt. Both books divide skills into categories associated with people, ideas, and things. People skills encompass interpersonal and intrapersonal abilities, ranging from friendly persuasion to conflict resolution, from self-assertion to self-management. Skills with ideas range from analysis to synthesis, from stringent focus to radical innovation. Skills with reference to things include the ability to manipulate and control, and to explore possibilities. In *We Are All Self-Employed*, Cliff Hakim likens skills to wild horses. You can't truly appreciate their value until they are corralled and harnessed.

Once we have a meticulous understanding of our skills and how we possess them in a hierarchical arrangement, it's easy to determine which ones we take with us from job to job and which ones we need to develop further for specific jobs or tasks. More importantly, we can see with greater clarity which skills we may refine with further schooling and which we may develop simply through continued effort and practice.

In *The Art of Using Your Whole Brain*, Katherine Benziger and Anne Sohn describe the way we knowingly look for ways to match our talents to the right job. Benziger calls it being driven by the smart-dumb rule: we naturally gravitate toward jobs and tasks that make us feel smart and away from jobs that make us appear dumb.

Think of how much easier and more productive the job search would be if we had prior objective knowledge about our talents and a practical understanding of the workplace so we could make a better match. Unfortunately we sometimes go far beyond the smart-dumb rule in that, when we find a comfortable fit with our thinking values, we tend to "live there." In other words, if the fit is with our work, we tend to become what we do, and exclude the areas we need desperately to appreciate but which make us uncomfortable.

After we gain enough self-knowledge to be able to confidently identify our talents, and after we understand enough about how organizations operate and how (following the whole-brain values model) our skills might best be used in that context, we are in a much better position to make career decisions. When we match our strengths to the task and the organization, we are capable of making our maximum contribution. At the same, time we'll know which areas of study to pursue for strengthening and broadening our skills.

Reputation

If your job was to hire a heavyweight prizefighter to represent your firm in fighting boxers hired by other firms, and the current heavyweight champion of the world walked into your office, would you demand to see a resume before hiring him? Of course not. Similarly, thousands of people move about in the workplace being hired by telephone or by message based solely on a reputation by being known as "the best at what they do."

When I was about 10 years old my grandfather turned 65 and retired from the Oklahoma oil field as a driller and tool pusher. He had earned such a reputation for being able to solve drilling problems (like fishing tools out of wells) that, for more than five years after he retired, oil companies called continually, pleading with him to go back to work or at least accept just one last assignment. I grew up thinking that the oil field was the easiest place in the world to go to work because they would just call you. Anyone who has tried to get a job in the oil field knows how hard it can be, but to have companies pleading with you to take a job or a special assignment means you have demonstrated your skills so convincingly that your reputation speaks for itself.

Consider how important it is to find a job that fits your interest and skills aptitude if you are to develop expertise to the point of establishing an exceptional reputation. A good reputation simply amounts to explicit proof of personal mastery. It carries with it the potential to overwhelm common perception, which is precisely what proving you are qualified depends upon.

Resumes

Thousands of people spend a lifetime changing jobs without ever having to rely on a resume, while others have never even considered trying to change jobs without one. Some misunderstand the use of resumes and expect too much, thinking that the resume by itself will play the primary role in getting them a job. A resume is simply a means of establishing a convincing argument that you should be considered as an excellent prospect for a job. An effective resume may capture the essence of a reputation for excellence, but its greatest use is to demonstrate to an employer that you have a great deal of potential. It should consist of a brief description of your education and work experience, with an emphasis on your accomplishments.

Creating a resume is worth the trouble, even if you don't use it, because it gives you an opportunity to focus clearly on what you want to accomplish. It's a way to pull together your strengths, posture, experience, skills, and reputation into a concise statement of purpose. This is not something you should hire someone to do, but something you should prepare yourself.

The two most popular types of resumes are the *chronological* resume and the *functional* resume. The chronological resume has been used for decades and is just what the name implies—a list of your experience and education in the precise order that it occurred. It is useful as an instrument to tell what you have done, but it offers little in suggesting what it is you want to do. A functional resume on the other hand makes a case for a specific job by offering a cogent argument as to why *you* should be selected.

I have been helping people write resumes for years, and the method I've found most effective is quite simple: Use a functional resume that begins with your name address and phone number, a clearly stated objective, a summary of qualifications consisting of about six specific reasons why your strengths are applicable the job (if indeed they are), followed by a short work and educational history emphasizing your accomplishments relative to your objectives. If listing the details of your education will not support your objective, as in the case of having dropped out of high school, then find a way to state the information in the most positive light possible, or leave the education section out completely. For example, you could list the year you passed the GED test or simply elaborate on practical (experiential) learning you've acquired, independent workshops you've attended, or hours of college credit you may have accumulated.

A crisp sense of self-knowledge, a working appreciation of all of your strengths, and well-defined goals and career objectives will better enable you to make a case that you are qualified. This can't be done in a day. It will take lots of time to read, reflect, and experiment. But the payoff in terms of clarity and direction will make it well worthwhile.

Learning with a Purpose

Being labeled as a high school or college dropout is a limitation only if you accept the label. As we've said, labels can limit or liberate. You are in control of the learning in your future, regardless of your current predicament. The very fact that you are reading this book is evidence that you refuse to accept the limitation of labels. Dropping out does not mean that you are a loser, that you are not intelligent, that you can't learn, or that you should in any way ask for less in life than you would have if you had graduated from high school or college.

Statistically, the consequences for remaining a high school dropout are that you can expect to earn 10 to 15 percent less in a lifetime than a high school graduate and from 35 to 40 percent less than a college graduate. In addition, you will have a much greater chance of remaining unemployed, while your options for different types of work will remain limited. In other words, you will have to settle for "jobs" while others select "careers." These are only statistics, however, and you are not a statistic. You still have a multitude of options for "dropping back in" to the process of qualification. You've already taken the first step by seeking to find out how.

GED

One practical way to finish high school without actually returning to school involves studying for and passing the GED test. General educational development testing (GED) began in 1942 as a war effort initiated to help assess the educational level of military service personnel. In 1952 GED testing was made available to civilians and is today accepted as evidence of a high school education in all fifty states.

GED standards are determined by the periodic testing of high school seniors who are about to graduate. In 1987, for instance, a national representative sample consisting of 20,000 twelfth graders was selected to take the test. Periodic testing ensures that the results of the tests remain current representations of educational standards. In reality, the completion of GED requirements offers a prospective employer *more* proof of competence than a high school diploma. For example, it is common knowledge that many students graduate from high school without being able to read, but the fact that you have taken the GED test and passed it is in itself evidence of your ability to read. It's also evidence of how well you measure up against others in your educational development.

Your approach to the GED test can be an act of rediscovering the intrinsic value of learning. The experience of preparing for the test can be a totally self-directed activity that will allow you complete command of the exercise. Once you learn to disassociate self-directed inquiry from the controlling aspects that accompany traditional education, you are on your way to discovering that self-education is the ultimate exercise in freedom. Pass the GED test, and you will prove to others that you have the knowledge expected of a high school graduate. Make the most of your preparation for the GED test. Use each study section to think through its relevance to your own life while you concentrate on developing the knowledge to pass the test. *You* are in charge. Enjoy it.

Another way to combat negative response to your not finishing high school is to change the focus from not having finished high school to that of having some college. After passing the GED, you need take only a few college courses to demonstrate that, while you may not have a degree, you can still do college-level work.

Vocational School

Vocational education seems like the obvious choice for many people without a college degree. No doubt, it is a viable option. Recognize, however, that vocational education or training is more often than not focused on a specific means to an end, such as a specific job, whereas self-education is a process that enables you to take charge of your own training. Also be forewarned that "vocational education in the schools for manual positions is virtually irrelevant to job fate."[7]

Vocational training opportunities exist in a vast array of disciplines. Vocational school marketing methods range from advertising on matchbook covers to accepting trainees only on a referral basis. From my own observations, I would estimate there are as many training rip-off schemes as there are legitimate opportunities, perhaps more. The rip-offs flourish precisely for the reason I stated earlier, namely that people in search of job training tend to be vulnerable. I suggest that, before you enroll in any vocational school, you make a thorough examination of the career field you are pursuing. Talk with people who are already in the specific type of job you plan to train for. Ask if a certificate from the training

school you are considering is really a respected credential. Find out
if there are opportunities to learn what you need to know as a
trainee or apprentice, in which case you could earn while you
learn, instead of paying to learn how to do a job that you may not
be able to get. Ask people with a lot of experience: where will this
industry be in five years or ten?

Traditional and Nontraditional College

People go to college for a multitude of reasons: some are genuinely interested in pursuing a particular field, some go to become
qualified, some go for the entertainment value, some go because
their parents insisted they go, and some go because it just seems
like the thing to do since everyone else is going. But for many
young people starting out in life, there is a sense of evaporating
time, a sense that four years is too long, that they must get on with
their lives and begin working. The older one gets, the more relent-
less a taskmaster time becomes, and the possibility of taking time
out to go back to school begins to seem ridiculous. Many people
believe they're too old for it.

The good news is that the times we are living in are changing
this paradigm. In *Managing for the Future,* Peter Drucker writes,
"For the first time in history it really matters whether or not people
learn." The realization that lifelong learning is a necessity is becoming more than a cliche. Moreover, there are more and more
options for continuing one's education. If going back to school is
important to you, if it has always been something you wanted to do
but didn't think you had the time, then ask yourself this question:
How old am I? If it takes two, four or six years for me to pursue the
formal education I want, how old will I be when I finish? Then, ask
yourself this question: How old will I be, in two, four or six years,
if I don't go back to school? My point is that it's almost never too
late to pursue more education if it is really important to you. And
today there are many ways to accomplish it.

Taking the traditional educational track in pursuit of a college
degree might make sense:

A. If you have already completed a large percentage of the
   classes you will need to graduate.
B. If you are still young enough that the socialization experience is important to you.
C. If money is no object.
D. If it is the only avenue available to develop credentials in
   your chosen field.

If you do choose the traditional route to obtain a degree, you'll find an abundance of good books on the subject at your local library.

More than a decade ago, in his book *Adult and Continuing Education*, Huey B. Long described four factors driving the acceptance of accumulative credits for long-term learning. They are:

> (a) a widespread public reevaluation of the worth of a college degree, (b) a strong movement toward providing educational credit for life experience, (c) an extended role for education in occupational recertification and relicensure, and (d) the emergence of consumerism coupled with the recognition of professional obsolescence.

These conditions have not abated but are smoldering today as the way in which adults are educated becomes fully engulfed in change.

Because colleges and universities owe their continued existence to student enrollment, they have little choice but to reach out to adults who are just beginning to realize they need help. The rise of nontraditional avenues to higher education is partly an admission that our current system is flawed, but it is driven more by demographics than by capitulation. There are five major reasons for the growth of nontraditional education:

1. Everyone involved in the process has long recognized that all learning does not take place in school and that attendance and passing grades are by no means in and of themselves proof of competence. Employers realize they have employees who have learned a great deal on the job with no academic certification to show for it.

2. Competition is fueling the demand for knowledge with such intensity that formal classes in distant institutions (which have always been slow to respond to change) simply cannot keep up. Documenting such cutting-edge knowledge as it occurs is easier than anticipating it and passing it on before it mutates. There is logic in rewarding people who can push the envelope of discovery. In contrast, it makes no sense to make their past achievements more important than their present ones.

3. A sharp drop in the birthrate from 1965 through 1980 and a dramatic rise in costs have meant that from 1983 through 1998 fewer students of college age have been available to attend college. It is fortunate that institutions of higher learning are having to rethink their objectives at a time when technological change is demonstrating that lifelong learning is a necessity.

4. Telecommunications are driving change. The availability of new forms of communication is analogous to the mountain climber who, when asked why he felt a need to climb the mountain, replied, "Because it's there." The "superhighway" capabilities of telecommunications, simply because they are there, are threatening to make traditional classroom attendance overly expensive and resourcefully obsolete.

5. Progress is changing learner needs. A constant climate of uncertainty stemming from technological advances has prompted thousands of adults to return to school to learn new skills or sharpen the ones they already have.[8]

Thus, nontraditional education has earned its name by adapting to the reality of the times we live in. Nontraditional education honors the notion that most learning takes place outside the classroom, that the demand for knowledge is escalating, that there are fewer students, and that the technology available today makes electronic transmission of information cheaper than the burning of fossil fuels necessary to get to a classroom.

Distance Learning

Distance education is really a euphemism for the electronic campus. Mind Extension University, founded in 1987 by Glenn R. Jones, serves as an electronic medium of delivery for a number of major universities, including the University of Alabama, the University of Arizona, the University of California, the University of Colorado, George Washington University, Kansas State University, the University of Maine, the University of Maryland, the University of New Orleans, the University of Oklahoma, the University of South Carolina, Utah State University, Washington State University, Western Michigan University and others. These institutions offer undergraduate, and graduate programs, as well as certificate programs and non-credit courses in a myriad of disciplines. Mind Extension University offers access to these institutions 24 hours a day. Courses are accessed electronically, students send in work by mail, and tests are administered by proctors near the students' locations. This method of continuing education offers the key of admission and the flexibility working adults need in order to participate. And this is only the tip of the iceberg. (See Recommended Reading for additional sources.)

In 1983, Huey B. Long issued a warning that should keep our attention well into the next century:

Competition among the purveyors of adult and continuing education will deepen. The competition will be manifested in several ways. It is predicted that "price wars" and "credential wars" will develop as institutions compete for selected markets. Increased proportions of budgets will be allocated for marketing. Educational institutions will follow the lead of business and profit-making firms by employing a staff of highly trained marketing personnel. Brochure copy and other publicity material will become highly sensationalized, and only institutions with the highest ethics will be able to withstand the temptation to promise more than they can be deliver.[9]

It's not my intention to throw cold water on the idea of nontraditional education. This is a system whose time, I believe, has come. Like any other business enterprise, however, it must be judged with discretion by those who use it. Someday I expect that Internet universities will offer certificate and degree programs which are closer in cost to magazine subscriptions than to today's astronomical tuition fees.

College Credit by Examination

College credit obtained through examination can be used in pursuit of both traditional and nontraditional degree programs. College-Level Examination Program (CLEP) tests are available for a vast range of subjects. Additional programs include the Advanced Placement Program (APP), and the American College Testing Program (ACT-PEP). These programs allow people with experiential learning to gain college credit by simply taking what might be considered the final exams. Your local book store, library, community college or university can furnish you with all of the additional information you need about examinations for college credit.

Portfolio Development

Portfolio development (sometimes called portfolio assessment or assessment of prior learning) is simply a concentrated effort to prove that your prior learning is worthy of college credit. It's as if you were building a case for a courtroom, trying to convince a judge and jury of your learned competence. Better yet, think of it as one of those television commercials where the competitor's product gets blown away. That's essentially what you need to do. Prove your learning beyond doubt. The following is but a partial list of the kinds of tangible evidence that can help you make your case.

A. What you've produced:
artwork
audio and video tapes
blueprints
brochures
computer programs
drawings
films

    lesson plans
    musical compositions
    patents
    photographs
    slides
    spreadsheets

B. What you've earned:
    awards and commendations
    letters from supervisors and associates
    licenses and certificates

C. What you've completed:
    college transcripts
    military service records
    past job descriptions
    reading lists
    research projects

D. Publications and speeches:
    articles in magazines or newsletters
    handbooks
    grant proposals
    newspaper items
    presentations
    reports
    resumes
    testimonials

The experience of documenting your life history is a highly instructive effort, even if you do not intend to continue to work toward a degree. It is a process few people would undertake without a strong reason, but it is a remarkable way to gain insight into how much you've already accomplished and what you really want to do with the rest of your life.

I completed a portfolio development program in 1986. The textbook we used was *Earn College Credit For What You Know* by Susan Sismosko. Our presentations for credit consisted of a goal statement, a resume, an autobiography, a competency worksheet, a competency statement, a reading list, a practicum, and a request for credit. These were put into large three-ring binders with as much support material from the tangible evidence list as possible.

Once compiled, a notebook like this could remain the primary source document for preparing resumes and presentations to help prove your qualifications in a myriad of employment situations. Computer graphics and desktop publishing techniques can make your presentation look very professional and offer compelling evidence of your prior learning. I have discussed this issue with personnel managers who admit to being extremely impressed with candidates who present such material for consideration during an interview. As you can imagine, the candidate who can furnish a life's worth of documented accomplishments compared to the one who just sort of shows up to be interviewed is likely to blow the competition away.

Documented accomplishment gives a prospective employer precise reasons to consider the candidate and to be confident that hiring this person would be less of a risk than hiring someone with potential but no track record. This premise is doubly true if you are seeking a promotion. What better way to dramatically alter your superiors' perception than to present a documented history of your accomplishments? Sometimes over-familiarity makes it very difficult for supervisors to penetrate routine appearances and realize that your current performance is indicative of much more capability. In this case, a well-presented portfolio may do more for you than a degree itself.

In a June 1992 issue of *Advertising Age,* retired advertising executive David Herzbrun (37 years of experience, 200 awards) wrote about his efforts to find a position lecturing and teaching at a college or university offering courses in advertising. His appeals were rebuffed because of his lack of academic credentials. One institution even returned a book he had authored because he lacked a doctorate degree. But, Herzbrun asks, "Has anyone in advertising ever known a practicing copywriter, art director or creative director who took the time to earn a Ph.D. in communication?" Herzbrun argues that trying to learn advertising from people with no practical experience is like trying "to learn cooking from a gourmet cook who has never been in a kitchen."

He further relates the story of a young man, just ready to graduate from a top communication school, who sought his advice about becoming a copywriter. Herzbrun asked to see the fellow's portfolio, which of course he did not have. In his pursuit of a very expensive degree, this student had never really created any advertising copy except for some headlines. But he had spent a great deal of time on "useless nonsense." A well-developed portfolio of your practical experience offers sage assurance that you have not spent your time engaged in nonsensical activities. Portfolio development courses are available from many colleges and universities (see Recommended Reading section).

The External Degree

In his book *Bear's Guide To Earning College Degrees Non-Traditionally*, John Bear suggests that the question of whether or not a college degree is worth the effort is "yes for a nontraditional degree; very likely no for a traditional degree." Bear writes,

> Much depends on the degree itself, and on the reasons for wanting it. If, for instance, a Bachelor's degree is required for a job, a promotion, or a salary increase, then the accredited degree of the University of the State of New York, earned 100% by correspondence courses, is exactly as good as any Bachelor's degree earned by sitting in classrooms for four or five or six years at a state university, and the cost would be less than 5% as much (not to mention that one can continue earning a living while pursuing the non-traditional degree).

More important than cost is the fact that seeking a degree in a field you are already interested in—one you already have experience in and an aptitude for—changes the picture entirely. Learning from such a posture makes far more sense for the student and for the discipline itself. If you are truly interested in your subject matter, if you are truly trying to add value in your chosen field, then a nontraditional degree program is an excellent way to go about it. What kind of approach could be more objective?

Objective Learning

Degrees themselves may offer little or no assurance of applicability to a particular workplace situation, but specific courses may be highly relevant to your job or circumstances. What kind of knowledge and expertise does your organization need? Are there classes available in the subject? If the answer is yes, does the discipline in question match your strengths? If the answer is yes again, why not approach your boss and make a case for sending you to the class? You could ask for some extra time, compensation, or special consideration for taking the course. Another approach is simply to ask the boss what kind of courses might help your organization gain a competitive advantage.

These are strategic actions. Determining what needs to be known and understood to meet the challenges of the future is what strategy is all about. If the areas suggested do not match your strengths, recommend that someone attend who is better suited. The lines are blurry in distinguishing where we learn what is worth knowing, but this is perfectly congruent with the way we live and work. In *Re-Inventing the Corporation*, John Naisbitt and Patricia Aburdine wrote:

The curious transformation of corporation into universities and universities into business is an analogue for what is going on in this society. We used to be able to divide our institutions into neat little boxes and say this is a bank, this is a retail store, this is a hospital, this is a business, and this is a school. But now we are erasing the lines that draw the boxes.

Indeed, we are erasing the lines of learning as well, even if we do not yet fully understand it. Perhaps, someday soon, we will realize that objective learning can occur anywhere.

Plan for the future

People from all walks of life are demanding educational reform. Many advocate a business and learning institution partnership where, with the cooperation of schools and businesses, students would be able to learn practical skills. While I am somewhat sympathetic with this view, I feel it is only proper if we balance classes of this kind with study which will enable us to continually keep business in perspective from the standpoint of our roles as citizens and creative beings, not just as employees. Regardless of whether you call it traditional education or vocational education, the thrust of all teaching in America needs to advance the idea, and cultivate the message, that business does not drive America, *citizens do*.

Purposeful learning lays the foundation for quality in every facet of work and for every enjoyment we experience in our personal lives. A determination to understand is what makes an uncertain future exciting.

Chapter Seven

Learning to Live
with Change

Acceleration is one of the most important and least understood of all social forces....A great deal of human behavior is motivated by attraction or antagonism toward the pace of life enforced on the individual by the society or group within which he is embedded. Failure to grasp this principle lies behind the dangerous incapacity of education and psychology to prepare people for fruitful roles in a super-industrial society.

—Alvin Toffler

Fundamental to my approach to self-education is the belief that personal maturation is dependent upon change. In his book *Future Shock,* Alvin Toffler painted a vivid picture of people coming apart at the seams because of their inability to cope with rapid change. My point is that the very process of self-directed inquiry is in and of itself a mechanism for coping with change.

Objective inquiry cannot help but reveal that we are biological beings. Self-education reestablishes our umbilical cord to the natural world and, in doing so, preserves our sanity. The resulting knowledge and understanding can counterbalance the technological know-how that is producing an artificial, sterile environment at breakneck speed. Left-brain thinking out of control drives us to future shock. The ability to achieve balance is always with us, if we have the presence of mind and the determination to look for it. The technology that allows us to probe deep space also enables us to look back at our own planet and observe the fragile, interdependent nature of our own existence.

The Nature of Change

Never in the history of mankind has the capacity for change been so great. Today, so many events call our attention to the possibility of change that we are desensitized. I've spent a lot of time searching for an original way to characterize the nature of change so that it seems real. The best I can do is to point out that, even though we think of ourselves as being accustomed to and therefore ready for change, when it actually occurs we say, "Yes, we were ready for change, but not this!"

Understanding change is key to being comfortable with the possibilities of the future. In his book *Mastering Change*, Leon Martel argues that understanding what is going on today, as most everyone else advocates, is not nearly as important as understanding the nature of change itself. He defines change as consisting of two components: *structural* and *cyclical*. Structural changes are permanent, such as the switch from the horse and buggy to the automobile. Cyclical changes come and go, as with the weather and the stock market. Knowing the difference between cyclical and structural change is essential to making intelligent choices.

If the field of work you choose is undergoing rapid change, you need to know if the changes are structural or cyclical. If you had gone into the harness business earlier in this century, you likely would have found yourself out of work. If, however, you had been a stockbroker during the 1929 crash, you still would have had a future in the field, even though you may have been out of work for a while. The difference today is that a structural change, such as the shift from horse to automobile, might nevertheless allow you to carve out a niche in the harness business. In other words, a local harness shop today could continue to thrive as a national mailorder outlet because of its ability to locate, identify and meet the needs of people who constitute its market.

An important part of developing a positive orientation toward the future is to fully realize that change is an opportunity for maturation and that we humans depend on the stimulation of change— not change in the sense of a treadmill of self improvements, but change understood in the context that all of life is change. No amount of denial, no avenue of escape, will still the fact that at this very moment we are growing and changing, cell by cell at a rate that strains our concept of mathematics. We are so perplexed by change, so off balance, that we fail to understand the paradoxical notion that while we need to grow, we also need to nurture our own youthfulness. People who dread the future lead unauthentic lives, fearing the very thing upon which they depend for growth. This is analogous to saying they are poisoned by their food. The irony is that most do not understand or consciously recognize where the real source of their discomfort lies.

People who fear the future resist change of any kind. They are prone to jump on the bandwagon of resistance by seeing conspiracies at every turn. They suspect everything they do not understand as being subversive to their way of life, while they make no effort to further their own self-understanding or to discover the true nature and cause of events. During times of rapid change, such people become fanatical for the familiar. Ethnocentrism becomes rampant.

Toffler warned us in *Future Shock* that, to survive, we must become infinitely more capable and adaptable. Capable, certainly, but I'm not so sure about adaptable. I might even assert the reverse. A large part of the problem is that we have already over-adapted to a system that is itself in dire need of changing. We must develop the ability and the political resolve to define and shape the nature of our structural system instead of bending to adapt to whatever circumstances come our way. The flip side to anticipating what skills will be needed in the future is a clear moral resolve about what needs to be done and in what context.

I believe Toffler is correct in saying there are limits to the amount of change people can endure, but that limit depends on one's posture. Knowledge about one's social and physical environment transforms raw stimuli into understanding; ignorance about one's social and physical environment turns those same stimuli into anxiety. Change—or the specter of it—has a much different impact on the psyche of those who feel they are clinging to a log swept aimlessly downstream than it does on the psyche of those who take it upon themselves to chart the course of their own vessels.

Our society has mastered the technology of wizards without reaching a parallel understanding of ourselves and of the responsibility such technology imposes. Only when we see that reality is a product of social construction, do we become overwhelmed with a sense of responsibility. We find that, to best serve humanity, complex technology must be driven by simple values.

When we borrow from the Buddhist principle of *Right Livelihood* we understand rationally and intuitively that our long- and short-term goals must not conflict. Short-term economics cannot be more important than the long-term condition of the environment. This does not in any way imply that economic necessity doesn't play a significant role in making practical decisions. Rather, it suggests that a multitude of people who care about the effects of their activities are as likely to be a force for positive change as any protest group. Organizations are much more easily changed from the inside than by external forces.

In his book *Powershift*, Alvin Toffler wrote, "The control of knowledge is the crux of tomorrow's worldwide struggle for power in every human institution." He argues that today's ever-accelerating rate of change is transforming the relationship between wealth and knowledge, revealing the very essence of power. To his mind, failure to understand the nature of these relationships is "a ticket to economic oblivion." Faced with such a threat, how can we hope to solve any of our serious problems, if we can't turn our moral resolve into political power and thus put our hands on the steering wheel of change?

Utilizing High Tech

Since its arrival in the workplace, the computer has found its way into every facet of American business. In fact, the computer has become the metaphor for technology itself.[1] For the vast majority of businesses in America, it's no longer practical to think of competing in the marketplace without one; it's no longer a matter of whether or not to purchase a computer, but rather what kind of "system" is necessary. In *Powershift*, Alvin Toffler observes:

> Anyone can see and touch the telephone or computer on the nearest desk. This is not true of the networks that connect them to the world. Thus we remain, for the most part, ignorant about the high-speed advances that are fashioning them into something resembling the nervous system of our society.

The computer is still feared and often completely misunderstood by people at all levels in our society, who as yet have no concept of a societal nervous system. One of the most important things to know about the computer is that there is no need to understand how it works in order to use it, but we do need to understand its effect on society. We never thought twice about the car's effect on society, and the damage resulting from that oversight is beginning to show.

Proliferation of computer technology sends confusing messages in all directions. In the simplest terms, it means that experience is reduced to data. For example, the popular term "hands-on" is often used to describe seemingly necessary work in many types of companies. This is replaced by a "hands-off" application when computer automation moves the worker from the production floor to the video screen.[2] For many who experience the change there is a feeling of alienation roughly equivalent to that of a dedicated soldier in wartime being transferred from the battlefield to headquarters. The worker, like the soldier, reacts initially with a feeling of helplessness, a sense that talents formerly acknowledged are not really being used, that there is no longer any way to make a contribution.

In time, this reaction will usually reverse, as the worker at the computer screen and the soldier assigned to headquarters come to the realization that this is where the power lies. The ability to influence the action far outweighs the disadvantage of not being on the front lines. Both the worker and the soldier will reduce their level of bodily effort, just as the soldier minimizes the risk of injury. The worker on the production floor is accustomed to using sensory information which, when based on years of experience, offers solutions to problems in ways that are difficult to explain: the worker just knows what is wrong and how to fix it.[3] With the move to the computer screen this sensory-based experience is lost. The hands-on approach is replaced by visual representations of letters, numbers, and graphs. A certain amount of time is required before such workers can establish an understanding of simple cause and effect. For example, can they trust what the computer says is true? How can they be sure?[4]

Transferring the knowledge gained from hands-on experience to a hands-off situation requires a more sophisticated level of understanding, which means learning more about the overall functioning of the system.[5] This amounts to a switch in brain dominance or thinking style as discussed earlier. For example, a floor production worker might favor a right-brain dominant thinking style, solving problems by imagery, intuition, and a general feel for the production process. Switching from the production floor to the computer terminal requires a switch, at least temporarily, to a more linear and logical left-brain thinking style. In time, though, a greater understanding of the system and processes at hand, and access to the information captured by the computing process, allow the worker to switch back to thinking with a right-brain orientation.

Computer scientists have become increasingly successful in creating programs called *virtual reality*. This is computer simulation of reality using visual imagery combined with the enmeshment of as many of the other human senses as possible. The more senses involved, the better the simulation. It is ironic that expectations foresee simulations more "real" than what we commonly call reality. Virtual reality will undoubtedly offer insight into how we might better inhabit ordinary reality.

Most of us grew up in America with a powerful understanding of what the term *diminishing returns* means and how it is an integral feature in the execution of capitalism. But technology and the insights of contemporary physicists in the science of complexity are now drawing our attention to "increasing returns."[6] In the technological marketplace, increasing returns account for such anomalies as the dominance of the QWERTY keyboard, which is inherently inefficient since it was designed to slow the process of typing to keep the key strikers from tangling. Thanks to increasing returns, VHS video recorder technology beat the superior Beta system. Increasing return is a phenomenon of momentum. Or, as physicist John H. Holland puts it, "Them that has gets."[7] Increasing return is a product of advantage, timing, and drive. These are profoundly important features of the high-tech marketplace, precisely because increasing returns are counter-intuitive to everything we have been taught about the way the world works. We have been taught that excellence wins simply because the best products stand out by virtue of their quality, not because they came along at the right time and gained so much market share that they overwhelmed better alternatives by sheer force. Though he was not discussing the concept of those who have getting more, William Bridges captured the essence when he wrote, "In a sense, everything about the world has a way of favoring the favored."[8]

Ideas vs Information

Data captured by the computer enable the process that Shoshana Zuboff, author of *In the Age of the Smart Machine*, calls *informating*—whereby the computer generates information that would otherwise have been unavailable or unnoticed. For example, compare a small business without a computer to one with an on-line computer database. The former puts old records and files in a storeroom and keeps active files in the front office. For practical purposes, all this is dead information. These records just take up space; they suggest nothing in the way of customer information unless they are pulled out and examined individually. Even then, they reveal very little, unless each is compared in some way with the others. But all the records in the company with the computer database are available at any time in a multitude of formats. Informating produces a mass of data for evaluation and analysis; it produces the kind of data that right-brain thinking thrives on.

In order to be creative, you first have to have something to be creative about. In other words, the power of the right brain must have stimuli to mesh with ideas to produce the effect we refer to as creativity. Theodore Roszak, author of *The Cult of Information: The Folklore of Computing and the True Art of Thinking*, has observed:

> . . . great mischief done by the data merchants, the futurologists, and those in the schools who believe that computer liter-

acy is the wave of the future: they lose sight of the paramount truth that the mind thinks with ideas not information.

I agree, the mind works with ideas, but until it acts on information with an idea, nothing happens. How does a society short on ideas respond to a deluge of information? Our lack of affection for ideas seems to explain at least partially why Richard Saul Wurman, author of *Information Anxiety*, would say, "the understanding business is virtually untapped." We need to appreciate the value of ideas as something separate from and greater than collected information.

Tangibles vs Intangibles

How do you personally relate to high technology? It can be extremely useful to review how your career priorities stack up and then consider how technology may influence or facilitate your achievement of them. Your attitude toward high technology is likely to have a great deal to do with how you see it affecting your ability to function in society. If you view technology as a threat, you would be wise to discover how to turn it to your favor. When you lay aside your emotions and apply yourself with a careful, well-reasoned approach, you'll realize there are many ways to make technology work for you. Once you reach a level of self-knowledge that points out exactly where your strengths and weaknesses lie, choosing high-tech components to amplify your performance becomes a very simple matter.

For example, highest on my priority list is my need to work independently. My desire to be free from organizations, and the possibilities of achieving that freedom, cause me to view technology positively. For me, the computer becomes an external left-brain. I am drawn to the aspects of technology that will allow me to achieve freedom. High-tech components mean that I am not location-dependent. The computer, together with telecommunications, the fax machine and cellular telephone, allows me to better control my day's work by saving me time and simultaneously offering me the freedom to work from anywhere in the world.

Still, this great advantage of technology, this fundamental strength, is also a weakness. In *Time Wars*, author Jeremy Rifkin says, "Statistics tell the grim story of a civilization hell-bent on saving time on the one hand while eliminating the future on the other." This weakness is a consequence not of hardware, but of people. We will be injured by this phenomenon only if we allow it to happen. The evolution of what we call work has continually moved us "farther and farther from the rhythms of nature."[9] Rifkin writes:

While the clock established the notion of artificial time seg-ments—hours, minutes, and seconds—it remained tied to the circadian rhythm. The clock dial was an analogue of the solar day, an acknowledgment that we perceive time revolving in a circle, corresponding to the rotation of the earth. In contrast, computer time is independent of nature: it creates its own con-text. A digital timepiece displays numbers in a vacuum-time unbound to a circadian reference. Computer time, then is a mathematical abstraction that attempts to separate us from the pulls and periodicities of the natural world.[10]

The importance of our own temporal orientation to the world is not so easily appreciated until you realize, as Rifken points out, "Every religion holds forth the prospect of either defeating time, escaping time, overcoming time, reissuing time, or denying time altogether."[11] Whether we attempt to stay umbilically bound to na-ture or become lost in abstraction among the nanoseconds is as much a political question as it is a career decision. The biggest difficulty is that we're not likely to acknowledge this as a problem until it becomes one of enormous proportions.

In *Powershift*, Alvin Toffler suggests that money and capital have changed from being tangible to symbolic:

> This vast sequence of transformations is accompanied by a deep shift of belief, almost a religious conversion—from a trust in permanent, tangible things like gold or paper to a belief that even the most intangible, ephemeral electronic blips can be swapped for goods or services.

Our wealth is a wealth of symbols. So also, to a startling degree, is the power based on it. Imagine what a deep shift in belief might do to a symbol-drenched work force. Think how hard it will be for people who do not understand the levels of abstraction in our lives to manage their own personal priorities. The more abstract our living becomes, the more we lose touch with the natural world around us.

The Future of Work

If you consider the amount of time humans have been on the earth in relation to the amount of time we have had what we for-mally call occupations, it is clear that what we consider "normal" in terms of work is anything but. The realization that we are one of the most stress-prone societies on the planet should render us spe-cifically sensitive to the fact that there might be better ways to ac-complish "work." The way we arise each day and travel long distances to work, reducing traffic in many cases to the earlier speed of the horse and buggy, is in itself suggestive that we can't lay claim to much in the way of progress. To earlier generations our modern-day antics would suggest that we are a nation of gypsies, wasting, in some cases, more energy to get to work than we accomplish at work. Many jobs today, in an entirely practical sense, do little more than offer the "comforting illusion that one is not getting something for nothing."[12]

The nature of work itself is constantly in a state of flux. We have gone from an agricultural society to an industrial one, and on to the loosely defined information society of today. Among the uneducated and uninterested, an information society might more appropriately be called an "informing society" because the instructive side of the information is entirely one-way. Being uninformed in an environment where the dynamics of information drive the very nature of society may add a whole new meaning to the notion disenfranchisement. An information society is a monolithic repository of data. For an information society to become a knowledge society means that the majority of people within society must be able to convert the data into new ideas.

John Naisbitt, author of the bestseller *Megatrends*, offers the terms farmer, laborer, clerk as a short history of the United States. The shift from each of these eras to the next is sharply punctuated by structural changes. We live in incredibly exciting times because an information society is so "fluid"—structural changes occur quickly, many times faster than during previous eras. We are now shifting from clerk to technologist. Today, lifelong education is a necessity just to keep in balance with or attuned to rapid change.

There are three areas that can help you detect change relative to your own work life. The first is to keep a close watch on social trends and demographics. Demographics are simply the numbers of and distribution of people in similar categories. For example, people born between 1946 and 1964 are called babyboomers because there were so many people born during those years (approximately 76 million). Babyboomers are watched closely by business because of their sheer numbers; they are prized as a highly valuable market. I believe that as we near the turn of the century, and babyboomers *en masse* reach their fourth and fifth decades of life, there will be a philosophical movement—reminiscent of the antimaterialistic philosophy of Henry David Thoreau and Ralph Waldo Emerson—that will make the "back to the land" movement in the 1970s look like a Sunday picnic.[13]

The study of social demographics may suggest the desires or predispositions of different groups of people. Second, adding the possibilities of high technical capability to the desires of different groups gives some insight into the direction of change. Third, and perhaps the most important area to study, are the changing relationships of power brought about by the new forms of knowledge processing. More specifically, ask whether the power is centralized (moving toward organizational control) or decentralized (toward individual control). Combine desires and possibilities of major population groups with thoughtful reflection about where the power really comes from, and you can develop a remarkably insightful orientation to the future. Then ask yourself, if a certain event occurred, would it be a structural change or a cyclical change? You can use this type of thinking to keep your career field in perspective.

It is not sufficient simply to be aware of your own strengths and skills while remaining unaware of what skills will be required for the future. To achieve equilibrium during times of rapid change requires a balanced perspective and the ability to anticipate—and retrain yourself to meet—new challenges, instead of being made obsolete by them. Many career counselors still preach job search techniques that were appropriate for the '60s and '70s without considering the structural changes in today's workplace. They tend to focus on job search strategies while ignoring the very real need to develop marketable skills.[14] Having solid, well-thought-out plans to prepare yourself for the future is one of the most impressive things you can demonstrate to a potential employer.

In an information-based economy, the ability and willingness to learn on the job are as important as the knowledge you bring to the job. In *Powershift*, Alvin Toffler offers the insightful conclusion that "knowledge—in principle—is inexhaustible—it is the ultimate substitute." For example, knowledge in the form of highly specific inventory requirements "is a substitute for both resources and shipping." Know-how allows a substitution of local versus distant resources; just-in-time inventory substitutes for stockpiling. The very characterization of a society that legitimately describes itself as a "knowledge society" represents the most profound change ever in the nature of work. In a knowledge society, the business concept of maintenance must be replaced with expectation for perpetual innovation.

For people, too, knowledge is the ultimate substitute: it is a good far greater than goods. For the first time in modern history, the worker can own his or her tools (the means of production) in a tool-kit of gray matter. The role of the organization in a knowledge society, according to Toffler, increasingly becomes that of an enhancer of the society's knowledge—a role which sends a clear message to workers that in order to add value in such an organization they must see to it that enhancement occurs within the organization.

The Importance of Finding the Right Fit

Finding the right fit early in your work life can affect whether you ultimately see yourself as a success or a failure. Trying many jobs, only to find they're not suited for the work, may cause some people to conclude they are failures at everything, when in reality they may simply have not found the right fit. Abraham Lincoln failed twice in business before he was 25 years old, had a nervous breakdown and failed in seeking public office eight times before becoming president. If he had given up after his first few bad experiences, we would never have heard of him.

The strongest message we receive in school is "fit or fail." No one explains that it's legitimate not to fit every situation. Contrary to what we've been taught to expect, if we don't fit a particular job or situation, the fault may not lie with us but with the job or organization itself. On a global scale, the state of our environment further suggests we are obsessed with trying to fit into a system which *itself* is radically in need of changing. When we are off balance in our personal lives, we're unlikely to have the time, the desire, or the power to make societal changes for the better. Unless our schools start delivering a new message, these necessary changes will continue to be neglected indefinitely. We don't need more people educated to fit into a broken society unless they also have the awareness and ability to help fix it.

Discovering our strengths and fitting into the workplace accordingly sounds perfectly logical and is one of the things this book recommends. This process, however, is not without its hazards: if we're not careful, our strengths are also likely to become our weaknesses. For example, a strength which requires a narrow focus can easily become a limited view during times of rapid change. This is precisely the argument which supports the case for lifelong education through continual self-directed inquiry. Narrow focus and specialization can contribute substantially to a feeling of helplessness because, without a broad view, we lose perspective. Gone is the sense of positive expectation that makes us receptive to the future.

The penalty for not finding out what we really want to do for a living, aside from the obvious economic waste, is that we are forever condemned to engage in tasks in which we lose interest. Our choice of occupation becomes uncomfortable; we run out of enthusiasm, often blaming ourselves for failure. If we had carefully considered our individual skills and aptitudes in the beginning, we might have concluded that we wouldn't thrive in this work, not because we were "failures," but because it was never an intelligent fit. Moreover, when our performance is judged in the workplace (which, more often than not is a counterproductive process in and of itself), we associate the act with that of being graded in school, except that now, instead of being good or bad students, we are considered good or bad people.

The task of self-education is to enable us to function within society by fitting in intelligently while developing the wisdom and sense of value necessary to define and build a better society. When you have developed self-knowledge to the degree that you can make intelligent occupational choices, you can make timely decisions with confidence, rather than having to surrender to the urgency of economic necessity.

Changing Careers to Keep Pace with the Times

The most dynamic characteristic of an information society is that many technological innovations promise rapid changes in the way we live and work. Telephones and televisions, personal computers, and satellites have brought structural changes which make it highly unlikely that we will ever return to lifestyles without such conveniences. Microelectronics add intelligent features to nearly every product we use. The net result is that the workplace itself is constantly changing. New businesses disappear as quickly as they emerge. Markets shift globally as the dynamics of world economics sort out who is in a better position to produce which types of goods. For you and me, this points to a need for changing careers much more often than we have been taught to expect. It means that we must learn to be comfortable with change. If we are to be effective in meeting our personal goals, we will have to rid ourselves of the archaic notion that education is something you can finish.

The need to frequently change careers means changing career strategies also; it's no longer sufficient just to appraise our strengths in terms of skills. During times of rapid change, it is also necessary to anticipate what skills will be needed in the near- and long-term future. Career search strategies for the future will require a switch from "Here is what I have done, may I please have the job now?" to "What kind of skills can I develop to ensure that I can help you solve problems in the future?"

An exciting aspect of a rapidly changing workplace is that occupations change faster than we can keep track of them. People find themselves engaged in tasks without titles. Rigid job descriptions dissolve because the nature of what has to be done is changing so quickly. This is especially true in highly technical fields, but it also applies to the service sector, which is the fastest growing segment of today's marketplace.

A large portion of the service sector is in a perpetual state of flux. The low end consists almost entirely of "temporaries," people who share the expectation that they are all on their way to doing something else. Thousands of service sector jobs have low entry-level requirements. But, for a few ambitious people with initiative and the demonstrated ability to learn on and off the job, the potential to move upward to much better paying positions is very good. At the higher end of the service sector are the workers perhaps best characterized as mind-workers, people who turn information into knowledge. These could be accountants, architects, engineering designers, bankers, educators, sales people, and government workers. Performance at the high and low end of the service sector affects customer relations. Meanwhile, technology continually increases choice, giving consumers a more significant role in the design of the products or services they purchase than they have ever had.

People who understand the times we live in and the nature of change in business have a decided advantage over those who do not. The temporary nature and low pay of many of the service sector jobs lead to poor performance and poor service. Service workers possessing a strong sense of purpose and objectivity, however, along with the people skills necessary to lead under such conditions, will have no lack of employment opportunities paying above-average salaries. Individuals who have clear ideas about what service really means and possess the ability to inspire others are rare and stand out easily among today's service workers. Indeed, they are beacons in a dark void.

Chaos and the Future

For as long as I can remember, well-meaning, concerned individuals have been talking about raising the standard of living in Third World countries. Today, living conditions in many developing nations are improving at the fastest pace in global history (although the disparity between haves and have nots is still catastrophic and growing larger). Now, many of those same well-meaning people are concerned that Third World improvements are out of control—out of control, they surmise, because their success *seems* to be coming at the expense of ours. As Third World countries gain jobs, America loses them. In spite of all of the faults attributed to capitalism (and there are many) the ashes of the Cold War have sprouted a "global marketplace."

The myth of American superiority is fading as we grope for perspective. This image calls to mind the ancient Greeks' view of time, as described by Robert M. Pirsig: "They saw the future as something that came upon them from behind their backs with the past receding away before their eyes."[15] Were it not for our myth-based notions of superiority and inflated egos, we might have been better prepared for the twenty-first century.

Today, as American manufacturing plants move to places like Mexico, we discover that jobs we thought could be performed only by high school graduates are handled easily by illiterate and semiliterate people after a little training. This does not mean that people don't need a high school education, but it does suggest we need to rethink our hiring practices and the entire process and concept of *qualification* and *opportunity*. In the past, when large numbers of uneducated people were out of work it was called at best a recession and at worst a depression. Now, when large numbers of educated people are out of work it is called a political disaster.

Many economists warn that we can no longer expect the stability we are accustomed to. We should have known better. It should come as no surprise that *capitalism means change*. There are profound economic shifts on the horizon which will dramatically alter the work and lifestyles of millions of people. And, in a way, it is the best news we've had for decades. It is an opportunity to question, to examine purpose, and to rethink what we are trying to accomplish through what we call work.

As we move into the uncharted waters of a chaotic economic future, it's important to realize that the discrete levels of reality in our ship's crew analogy are becoming blurred and less functional. To extend the metaphor, we increasingly find ourselves in the same boat, and we move closer to realizing that even the lowly deckhands have a legitimate say in choosing the destination of the ship, controlling the burnt fuel residue which spews into the air, and curbing the waste we throw overboard. Slowly we are becoming aware that our methods are not more important than our reasons for having them, which is simply another way of saying that form is not more important than substance.

Flattening the pyramid, downsizing, and the structural changes coming about through a democratizing phase of capitalism are leading us deep into new territory. Although these efforts which seem to promise a more democratic workplace may appear to be noble, they have nothing to do with ideology. Rather, they are the result of expanded competition, period. And, in spite of the fact that now is a good time for rethinking our original purposes, it is also a time of intense anxiety. The implications are glaring that we are moving further and further toward a decisively split society with razor sharp distinctions: people with careers versus people with jobs; haves versus have nots; knows versus know nots; rich versus poor; and those with political power versus those without. The history of human beings on this planet has left a clear record of the troubles to which these types of inequity lead. It is bewildering to watch good paying jobs vanish, whether we call it flattening the pyramid, downsizing, or restructuring, or whether we attribute the cause to economic efficiency, global equity, or corporate greed.

We are moving rapidly toward a society that resembles an hourglass. The stem in the middle separates a group in the top half, which faces a bright economic future, assured of being treated more and more like adults, from the group in the bottom half, which will be treated more and more like children. In fact, the hourglass model itself may soon become larger at the bottom than the top. In 1959, the top 4 percent of Americans earned as much as the bottom 35 percent. By 1989, that ratio had shifted to 4 percent and 51 percent.[16] Moreover, a recent census study found that 18 percent of full-time workers in America earn less than $13,091 per year. Short of a political revolution, the era of high-wage, low-skill jobs is gone forever.

The size of the American economic pie has remained constant while the share going to the so-called professional classes has grown larger and larger. It would seem that Ivar Berg was correct when he wrote, "Policies calculated to generate job opportunities for a growing population would seem to deserve higher priority than those designed to rationalize, by their stress on education, the considerable difficulties imposed on those without academic credentials."[17] The future of democracy may depend upon some new recipes which focus less on the redistribution of wealth and more on the redistribution of opportunity. The vast majority of Americans have long subscribed to the notion that, if everyone just had more education, the economy would straighten up and fly right. This long-held myth, if not now shattered, is at least fractured. One clear result of higher education is that it leads to instantaneous dissatisfaction with low wages, which may result in a political backlash. Downsizing has created an unemployment structure where thousands of people accustomed to sharing power now find themselves powerless.

American history is rife with examples of doomsayers who have met each period of structural change with prophecies of ruin and destruction. I don't care to join them, but to deny that we face the potential for cataclysmic social unrest in this country is to deny the obvious. Communication and biotechnologies promise a future of possibilities that we can barely comprehend, just when it seems we must face the fact that a large part of our work force has become redundant. Despite all of the rhetoric about an exponential explosion in the number of high-tech jobs on the horizon, there is little sign that they will actually appear. Indeed, in the very near future, the question of social equity is going to loom much larger than how well we are meeting global competition.

Two hundred years ago, British economist Thomas Malthus argued that populations would always outrun food supplies, resulting in perpetual world hunger. By all appearances, Malthus would seem to be correct, but, in truth, there *is* enough food to feed the world (though maybe not for long). It is political power that does not keep up with population growth. This, of course, is by design. When people obtain power, they do not easily let it go. The powers of production have, in fact, improved so dramatically that, where once most of the people in America were in some way connected to an agrarian economy, today it takes less than three percent of the population to feed us, with a surplus left over for export. Industrialization is moving in the same direction, and so is what we are today loosely calling the service sector or information economy. We are continually doing more with less, as information substitutes for inventory and labor.

In his book *The End of Work*, Jeremy Rifkin writes,

> In recent years, scores of futurists have written breathless tracts prophesying the end of history and our final deliverance into a techno-paradise mediated by free-market forces and ruled over by detached scientific expertise....The predictions are not without merit. We are, indeed, experiencing a great historic transformation into a third Industrial Revolution and heading inexorably toward a workerless world....The very notion that millions of workers displaced by re-engineering and automation of the agricultural, manufacturing, and service sectors can be retrained to be scientists, engineers, technicians, executives, consultants, teachers, lawyers and the like, and then somehow find the appropriate number of job openings in the very narrow high-tech sector, seems at best a pipe dream, and at worst a delusion.

Short of a global catastrophe, I doubt that the next few decades will see the literal end of the traditional job, but in a metaphorical sense I believe Rifkin is on the right track. As much as I've read and studied on these issues, I am unaware of anyone who has made a clear, compelling case that the future will offer economic opportunities to sustain a growing middle class in the manner it has become accustomed to expect. This is not due to a lack of interest. On the contrary, the demand to make economic sense out of the fast times we are living in has experts in every field scrambling to explain what is ahead. I believe what little evidence there is suggests that the future will require us to rethink the nature of work and reexamine the social contract of citizenship in America. This rethinking calls for a whole new approach to organizing our resources to deal effectively with economic and social issues. In *Jobshift*, management consultant William Bridges writes,

> The job is a social artifact, although it is so deeply embedded in our consciousness that most of us have forgotten its artificiality or the fact that most societies since the beginning of time have done just fine without jobs....Before people had jobs, they worked just as hard but on shifting clusters of tasks, in a variety of locations, on a schedule set by the sun, the weather, and the needs of today. The modern job was a startling new idea—to many people, an unpleasant and even socially dangerous one. Its critics claimed that it was an unnatural and even inhuman way to work....Americans even once talked about the job as "wage slavery" and contrasted it with the farmer's and craftperson's freedom and security. But what started as a controversy became the ultimate orthodoxy: we're hooked on jobs.

Hooked indeed, politicians who have little understanding of the chaotic times we are living in, and even less of the history of work, promise (if elected) to produce jobs as if the task were as simple as pulling rabbits from a hat. But before anything like an economy exists where there is plenty of work to do but no formal job designations stating who does what, there will have to be a great rethinking about how we are to live: how we'll finance homes, cars, and a vast range of services from health care to transportation.

This rethinking process can appropriately begin with the question of credentialism: what work is to be done, and who is qualified to do it? The downsizing and reengineering of corporate America is being followed by similar demands of government. If these restructuring pressures continue, policies which focus more on performance and less on academic standing can't be too far behind. In a knowledge society the lore of business is too chaotic for learning institutions to keep pace. Moreover, the very definition of an educated person will change with the times. Learning will become more and more the province of the individual. Of course, the reverse could obtain: formal credentialism could become more entrenched than ever. But when knowledge *itself* becomes the backbone of the economy and proves more important than the production and distribution of goods, then *what* a person knows becomes truly more important than *whom* they know. What they do and how they perform *really matters*. This means businesses will need knowledge workers more than the workers will need them.

Such a reversal of fortune will advance my thesis into an ever-increasing reality: that an education should be not something you *get*, but something you *take*. Thus, the capitalism of education will mean that learning will be more consequential than ever, but how one's knowledge is acquired will be of little concern. One's current level of interest in a subject will be far more important than a distant familiarity. But to position oneself to take advantage of expeditious change requires a whole new sense of personal organization.

Chapter Eight

Me, Inc.

*The most productive people tend to be students all their lives.
Discovering and developing new facets of their potential excite
them the way mastery of a sport excites an athlete, particularly
when mastery increases the speed at which improvements occur.*

—Charles Garfield

The Learning Organization and the Learning Individual

One of the best ways to fight credentialism at a practical level is to rise above it by developing genuine expertise in your own field and in your own life. We are swamped with information today, but knowledge is as hard to come by as it has ever been. Our credential-dedicated society comes with the answers built-in. There has been so much focus on answers in order to meet the requirements of qualification that it is no longer common to ask questions about matters considered settled by the majority. It should not come as a surprise, then, that there is no better guiding principle for developing expertise in your own field than to learn how to ask the right questions.

The first thing we have to do is give ourselves permission not to know. Author of *Information Anxiety*, Richard Saul Wurman, captures the twisted character of a credential society by suggesting, "We live in fear of our ignorance being discovered and spend our lives trying to put one over on the world." This is a common stance in many organizations where people fear letting on that there is anything they do not thoroughly understand about their work. This phenomenon is common not just at the lower levels of the organization; it often gets worse the higher one goes. Downsizing compounds the problem.

The great tragedy is, if we weren't afraid to formulate probing questions, not only could we solve our immediate problems, we could reach the very core of quality of life. Questions mold the foundation of learning. I once heard the great motivational speaker Earl Nightingale say that by spending one hour a day studying one's main field of interest, a person can in a short time become an expert. I believe he was correct. You can use this method to easily become the most knowledgeable person in your area of interest within in your own organization—if for no other reason than the fact that few people maintain a high level of curiosity about their work, at least not yet. "Interest," Wurman says, "defies all rules of memorization." Wurman submits that our educational system should integrate knowledge between disciplines. He writes,

> I've proposed that we should have courses taught by five profes-
> sors around one topic. For example, five professors teaching
> together, not lecturing at each others' class. A course on the
> cosmos to be taught by a physicist, a biologist, a geologist, a
> philosopher, a mathematician.[1]

I quote Wurman's proposition to emphasize that when we give ourselves permission not to know, when we stoke the coals of our own interests, there is absolutely nothing to keep us from bringing this kind of approach to any question that comes to mind. We can ask the opinion of five, or twenty, knowledgeable people if we so desire. Thus, we can fight credentialism by playing in an arena so foreign to those who try to hide their ignorance that we win by default. It's ironic that, in organizations where people are particularly sensitive to their lack of knowledge, the person who readily admits ignorance isn't regarded as a threat.

Nothing I have said in this book is more important than this: the greatest power that you and I have as individuals is *the power to define value for ourselves*. If you remember nothing else, do not lose this message. The greatest price we pay for not studying history is to think that the way things are is the way they have to be. History is rife with evidence to the contrary. In most any circumstance, there is always a robust need for people who readily take responsibility for their own learning, who have a strong sense of purpose, who ask important questions, who assume responsibility without passing on blame, and who choose a life posture of self-reliance.

In his book *The Fifth Discipline: The Art and Practice of the Learning Organization*, Peter Senge identifies five disciplines necessary for creating and maintaining a learning organization:

1. **Systems thinking** is a prescription for seeing wholes and understanding relationships, especially interrelationships.

2. **Personal mastery** is a sense of personal responsibility for understanding and meeting individual and organizational needs now and in the future. Personal mastery is a sense of commitment that ensures its own confidence. The adoption of an attitude of personal mastery is the essence of the attitude toward education itself: that an education isn't something that's done to you, but is something you deliberately seek out.

3. **Mental models** form our sense of reality. They are templates, paradigms, and programs. Understanding mental models means understanding how we understand and how the way we see the world often keeps us from understanding it better.

4. **Shared vision** is the manifestation of a deep understanding of what everyone is trying to accomplish. Shared vision is born of communicated purpose.

5. **Team learning** requires that the individuals within an organization continually engage in dialog and practice in carrying out the objectives of the first four disciplines. Synergy (evidence that the whole has become greater than the sum total of its parts) is the product of team learning.

Just as these components constitute what is needed for a learning organization, they are also what is needed to produce the learning individual. In times of rapid change, we need to understand whole relationships in order to make sense out of chaos. We need personal mastery to rise to the occasion. We need to recognize the models through which we have come to understand our old world so that we may change them, if necessary, to better understand reality and to create a more suitable new world. A shared vision is what pulls us along. If each of us approaches these four disciplines with a commitment to sharing our knowledge and experience, we can learn as a team. The everyday world we live and work in is analogous to a journey into uncharted waters. Too bad that so many of us do not realize this until the day we wake up discover our world no longer makes sense.

Specialization

No subject has been more confusing during the past twenty years than whether or not Americans should become specialists or generalists. In his book *Post-Capitalist Society*, management consultant Peter Drucker makes this issue crystal clear:

The prototype of the modern organization is the symphony orchestra. Each of the two hundred fifty musicians in the orchestra is a specialist, and a high-grade one. Yet by itself the tuba doesn't make music; only the orchestra can do that. The orchestra performs only because all two hundred fifty musicians have the same score. They all subordinate their specialty to a common task. And they all play only one piece of music at any given time.

This analogy helps clear up one of the most perplexing aspects of the need for specialization. Drucker continues,

> We surely overdo specialization these days, worst of all in Academia. But the cure is not to try to give specialists a "liberal education" so as to make "generalists" out of them (as I used to advocate myself for many years). This does not work, we have now learned. Specialists are effective only as specialists—and knowledge workers have to be effective. The most highly effective knowledge workers do not want to be anything but narrow specialists. Neurosurgeons get better the more they practice their skill; French horn players do not take up the violin, nor should they. Specialists need exposure to the universe of knowledge. . . But they need to work as specialists and to concentrate on being specialists.

Indeed, much of the confusion over this issue arises because specialists tend to value only their own area of specialty. But, using the orchestra analogy, it's not hard to show that we must value all of the instruments, if we really want to play and to hear beautiful music. Only when we understand the importance of our own specialty, can we truly appreciate the value of all of the others.

In an information-rich environment, generalists can act more like specialists, and specialists, through the use of their autonomy, can act more like generalists. Traditionally, when an orchestra performs, the members play at the same time in precise harmony. In today's dynamic organization, however, the music is more like improvisational jazz: each player decides not only when to play but with whom, for how long, and how loud. The quality of the performance rests in how satisfactorily the total score rings true in the ears of the customers. Thus, the players are more interdependent than ever, and their appreciation for one another can only improve. That's why the whole-brain model mentioned earlier is so useful. It offers a clear method of valuing *all* of the diverse personalities, natural talents, affinities, and predispositions which make up the human race. This lesson bleeds through to the very fabric of human relations.

Entrepreneurs and the Ground Floor

Getting in on the ground floor is a term most often used in reference to investment opportunities. But the ground floor is also a terrific place to work. Small companies provide most of the new jobs created each year. In his book *Global Paradox*, John Naisbitt writes,

> Only 7 percent of U.S. exports are created by companies with 500 or more employees. The Fortune 500 now account for only 10 percent of the American economy, down from 20 percent in 1970. Ninety percent of the U.S. economy is elsewhere: small and medium-sized companies. Entrepreneurs—individuals— are creating the huge global economy.

Moreover, new business ventures are most often started by visionaries. And visionaries, by their very nature, pay more attention to enthusiasm and genuine talent than they do to rules about who has the right paper credentials. If you share their vision, their interests, and their enthusiasm you may also share a place in one of their organizations. Peter M. Senge writes, "If people don't have their own vision, all they can do is 'sign up' for someone else's. The result is compliance, never commitment."[2]

The most difficult aspect of getting in on the ground floor is being in the right place at the right time. And the only way to be in the right place at the right time is to investigate your field of interest to such an extent that you can speak to a visionary as a visionary. Large organizations often stifle creativity by nature of their design. Small organizations flourish on creativity. The thesis of the book *Global Paradox* is based upon Naisbitt's premise, "The bigger the world economy, the more powerful its smallest players."[3] Imagine the deal someone with an aptitude and burning desire to work in electronics could have made, had that person found Stephen Jobs and Steve Wozniak while they were still making Apple computers in their garage.

It's not surprising that one of the traits successful entrepreneurs share is a dislike for highly controlled, structured environments like school. In *The Question Is College*, Herbert Kohl points out that "most family fortunes were initially made by people who never spent a day in college." Entrepreneurs are individuals in business for themselves. By its very nature the proposition is an act of independence. A check into the background of accomplished entrepreneurs will reveal that many were not successful in school, but the very reasons they were not made them winners in business.

Billionaire Ross Perot stops just short of saying ignorance is a virtue to the entrepreneur, in claiming that determination and persistence are far more important traits than intelligence. In his opinion, the smarter you are, the more sensitive you are, and you need to be dumb enough not to quit. Ever. (He said this before the 1992 presidential election.) Entrepreneurs continually do things contrary to what everyone else seems to think is possible. After they have done so, their actions will be considered absolutely normal, offering support to the premise that "people who don't know they can't, do."

Opportunities for entrepreneurs are not restricted and blocked at every turn for want of a credential. To be a successful entrepreneur you still need competence—it just doesn't matter whether you gain that competence by hiring someone with the necessary expertise or by figuring things out for yourself. Becoming a successful entrepreneur simply requires that your expertise, however acquired, doesn't let your grasp exceed your means. In other words, don't pay out more than you take in. Self-education to the entrepreneur is simply a method of minimizing risks by learning and knowing what you are doing. These are "the best of times and the worst of times" for entrepreneurs. They are the best of times because of rapid change. They are the worst of times for the same reason.

Strategic Learning

Simply put, strategic learning requires a strategy. And, while this is not an earthshaking revelation, the undertaking requires considerable effort. What business owner or manager would not be excited about a work force so intently interested in their enterprise that they anticipated knowledge and skills that would be needed in the future and planned with management and among themselves to acquire them?

Traditional education has provided the workplace with a continual stream of "good" students whose primary motivation was dependent upon what the teacher wanted. It is thus not surprising that a great many of these people are not, by experience, notoriously independent thinkers. Now, as independent thinkers are beginning to be needed more and more, organizations don't even know how to treat them because independent thinkers don't, as a rule, act like good students.

Learn to reflect strategically without appearing to threaten the hierarchy, and your value in the eyes of your organization is likely be dramatically enhanced. Learning to think strategically in chaotic times requires that we start seeing ourselves less as employees and more as resources—resources which can be expanded and leveraged. Such strategies acknowledge that if the primary usefulness an employee provides to an employer becomes infrequent, then that employee will be eliminated in favor of a contracted service. In other words, if an employee who is a welder spends only part of the time welding, it will be cheaper to pay a contractor on an on-call basis than to keep a full-time welder on the payroll. Strategic thinkers don't view this as a job loss, but as an opportunity to provide a service for a fee higher than an hourly wage.

Strategic thinking requires an understanding that all endeavors with a life span have an upward and downward cycle. The time to change—the time to move in a new direction—is *before* your current upward trajectory begins to slip and turn downward. It's like trading in your car while it's still in good shape to ensure you get the best possible price and to avoid the hassle when it begins to fall apart. This kind of vigilant awareness is becoming more and more crucial to the long-term success of businesses and individuals alike, but it is increasingly hard to do, because it often means stopping or quitting an activity while it is still successful. It seems counter intuitive to get rid of a good car, until you consider how little value it will have when it's worn out, and what a headache an unreliable vehicle can be. Television producers have learned that canceling a long-running TV series while it's still popular will ensure greater revenues from rerun syndication rather than waiting until the public tires of the program. In other words, you're more valuable when you're in top form than when your abilities are waning. This kind of thinking is an acknowledgment that change, learning, and growth are synonymous.

High-Tech Leverage

In every organization of any size there is a greatly overlooked area where you can proceed to anticipate the future of your field— namely, exploring the unused technological potential currently available. Take stock of the equipment the business already has on hand—the telephones, fax machines, copy machines, the computers and software—and start using it to its full potential. If the features in use so far were subtracted from the equipment's full capability in dollar figures, the difference would be startling. I know from my own experience working in a Fortune 500 company that only a fraction of the conveniences created to enhance productivity are actually being used. Employees at all levels and departments are guilty of this oversight. Why? There are numerous reasons. In some cases, these features have sort of crept into the organization unannounced. In others, they have arrived all at once. While many of us were paying little attention, for example, the telephone became a multifaceted communication device.

The bottom line is, if these technological advances are applied as intended, they will add significantly to the efficiency and the effectiveness of any individual or organization who will put them to use. They amplify the power of the individuals and the organizations who take advantage of them. Moreover, familiarity with these technologies would give you the benefit of insight into the state of the art in your field and to possibilities that are not yet obvious to the majority of employees.

While many of these devices appear overly complicated, most are not—if you take into consideration that they have been designed by people who prized technical qualities more than the need to explain them. Even the equipment that appears too complex is often easy to learn, given a willingness to invest some time and patience. If necessary, you can call the manufacturer and talk to the engineers personally. (Nobody has to see you do this.) Take the manuals home, spend a few weekends mastering these devices, and it will transform your attitude about technology. Especially as technology tackles more complicated tasks, those committed to keeping up with new developments will gain increased feelings of confidence and greater respect from their peers.

The point missed by so many regarding high-tech leverage is that technology is nothing more than a tool—a tool which enables creative and innovative people to get results, regardless of whether or not they themselves are technically oriented. William A. Schaffer, author of *Hi-Tech Jobs for Lo-Tech People*, writes,

> For those of you who have a background in liberal arts and have had a rough time finding a really good, satisfying job, one that meets your expectations and challenges you to grow intellectually and emotionally, I have a really good piece of news: The high-tech industry *needs people like you*.

The irony here is that many people running high-tech industries have been slow to realize technical tools are useless unless one has a purpose in mind for using them—a purpose which can be oblivious to understanding the technical nature of one's tools. Cars would have little value if people had no wish or need to travel. Moreover, people use cars every day without having the slightest idea about how they work. Purpose must be leveraged if technology is to be utilized effectively. In simple terms this amounts to:

$$\text{Me, Inc., x high-tech = leverage.}$$

For far too long, most of us have used the reason that we are not technically oriented as an excuse to let technology get ahead of us. This pretext is becoming less and less acceptable, and rightly so. The management of an organization which invests millions for the latest technology can justifiably expect it to be used effectively. Sadly, managers are sometimes the most fearful of new technology. But don't let that stop you—the initiative you take to bite the technological bullet could make your employer more competitive.

The Me, Inc., Philosophy

In the *Independent Scholar's Handbook,* Ronald Gross writes,

What independent scholar has not been confronted with the officious secretary's query: Who are you with? Once America was known as a nation where institutions were understood to be merely the lengthened shadows of the individuals who created and composed them. Today the reverse is the case: Individuals derive their legitimacy, in many people's eyes, from the shadowy institutional aegis under which they operate.

With this in mind, I propose that, in defense of our power to define our own reality, we henceforth think of ourselves as Me, Inc. America began as a nation that way, didn't it?

Scarcely more than a century ago, most Americans lived on farms. Living was hard. Life was short. But there was an element of independence and self-reliance that later generations have never fully understood. These early Americans were deeply aware that they were 100 percent responsible for the value their work added to their fortunes. The massive industrialization which took place in the 1890s and beyond offered a new compact: self-reliant individuals could exchange their independence for employment security. Responsibility gradually gave way to obedience and conformity, as uniformity overshadowed initiative. Industrialization was taking place at a time when agriculture was suffering from diminishing returns. Settlers were increasingly choosing land which was unsuited for farming, which meant that hard work was increasingly becoming a feature of poverty. People left farms in droves to seek employment. Cash currency replaced an exchange of goods and labor which constituted the core of community. The new employment compact implied a reciprocal loyalty which was often more apparent than real. In little more than a century, America went from a nation of predominantly self- employed individuals to a nation of employees, who became far more dependent upon an abstract economy than farmers had ever been on the weather.

Today, the core of community has evaporated into an ethos of self-interest which holds little regard for the interests of others. The "Me Generation" of the '70s has been disparaged as a low point of the century. Now, however, we must admit that the most appropriate posture for individuals relative to employment during the

'90s is a "Me, Inc." attitude. In reality, it has always been that way: the unspoken presumption of reciprocal company loyalty was rarely more than an illusion. The needs of today's organizations are changing almost as quickly as technology itself. A Me, Inc., posture is not a product of self-absorption, but rather is a return to the realization that each of us is 100 percent responsible for the value we create. Me, Inc., assumes a stance of self-reliance, a sentiment of personal mastery. Anyone intent upon anticipating the needs in any field today must set out to learn everything possible about it. In *The Fifth Discipline,* author Peter Senge writes,

> People with a high level of personal mastery share several basic characteristics. They have a special sense of purpose that lies behind their vision and goals. For such a person, a vision is a calling rather than simply a good idea. They see "current reality" as an ally, not an enemy. They have learned how to perceive and work with forces of change rather than resist those forces. They are deeply inquisitive, committed to continually seeing reality more and more accurately. They feel connected to others and to life itself. Yet they sacrifice none of their uniqueness. They feel as if they are part of a larger creative process, which they can influence but cannot unilaterally control.

We can't control the future, but we can be assured of getting the most from it if we adopt a posture of personal mastery. We can use mental models, shared vision, and systems thinking with the realization that the quality of our lives and the quality of the society we live in are directly dependent upon our own individual sense of responsibility. Ivan Illich puts this in perspective with regard to credentialism:

> The waning of the current professional ethos is a necessary condition for the emergence of a new relationship between needs, contemporary tools, and personal satisfaction. The first step toward this emergence is a sceptical and non-deferential posture of the citizen towards the professional expert. Social reconstruction begins with a doubt raised among citizens.[4]

This is the responsibility contour of Me, Inc. If we do not press for rational policies with regard to a credentialed society, we diminish the quality of our own lives and that of society itself. Illich continues:

> The Age of Professions will be remembered as the time when politics withered, when voters guided by professors entrusted to technocrats the power to legislate needs, the authority to decide who needs what and a monopoly over the means by which these needs shall be met. It will be remembered as the Age of Schooling, when people for one-third of their lives were trained

how to accumulate needs on prescription and for the other two-thirds were clients of prestigious pushers who managed their habits. It will be remembered as the age when recreational travel meant a packaged gawk at strangers, and intimacy meant training by Masters and Johnson; when formed opinion was a replay of last night's talk-show, and voting an endorsement to a salesman for more of the same.[5]

In essence, proving you are qualified means taking back some of the power and quality of life that has been lost to credentialism. It means thinking of your talents and skills as strengths, as capital assets, which must be continually developed and upgraded. Proving you're qualified means turning your anger at the injustice of credentialism into strategies for positive action. The concept of portfolio development works nicely for educational credits, but it is a fundamental strategy in a Me, Inc., mindset. A Me, Inc., perspective requires acknowledging new workplace realities: businesses built around a small core of knowledge workers, in flattened hierarchies, relying on contractors and ad hoc alliances for services and labor.

If Me, Inc., were a large company its structure might be organized around the principles and strategies set forth in this book. The accompanying diagram illustrates how the organization might look. The arrangement of your own organization of course, is up to you. You are the president and chairman of the board. You're better off creating your own design than borrowing mine. You may want to discern your objective, or your bottom line first and then adjust your resources accordingly. Knowing you possess a vast reservoir of viable resources is pivotal to the perceptual changes necessary to make a go of Me, Inc.

What I have called Me, Inc., William Bridges, in his book *Jobshift*, has characterized as You & Company. Bridges uses the apt acronym D.A.T.A., to stand for your desires, abilities, temperament, and assets. Once you begin to think of yourself as a source of continually upgradable skills and valuable services, the task of proving you are qualified is cast in a new light. And if you have an adequate understanding of credentialism, the action steps you need to take will appear obvious.

Changing Minds

In contemplating what it takes to change minds, we can take a lesson from the white knight theory, affirmative action, and gender bias. To change minds is to change perception, and the sensory information needed for this must be overwhelming. It takes little reinforcement to maintain the views we already hold, but it takes a

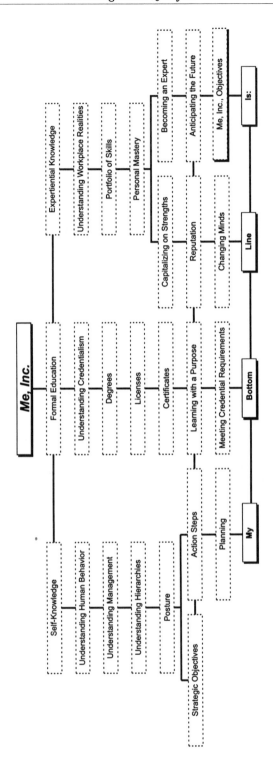

tidal wave of hard data and personal experience to compel us to change our minds. That's why bigotry and prejudice are so easy to pass from one generation to the next. For someone to be seen as the obvious choice for promotion, the evidence in favor of that person must be self-evident, just as excellence is recognizable in athletes and musicians, and genius was recognizable in Einstein's physics. Admittedly, being promoted to the next level in most organizations does not require feats equal to producing the formula for relativity, but to be seen as unequivocally the right choice for promotion requires the same kind of perception. A promotion is based, not on what we ourselves think, but on what *someone else* thinks.

The manager searching for the white knight outside of the organization has a mental notion (in most cases unrealistic) of someone with exceptional abilities, precisely because no one within the organization has been *recognized* as possessing such extraordinary skills. In other words, idealistic expectations and limited awareness are at work simultaneously. An effective way to alter such perception is to overpower it.

Think about how many times you have changed your mind on important issues during your life. It's hard to pin down the specific reasons why we suddenly reverse our opinions. The shift in mind either happens slowly like a snowfall gaining the momentum of an avalanche, or it happens all at once like an earthquake. We never go back and look for evidence of what it was that started the avalanche or the strain and tension that triggered the quake. Once our minds are changed, we may become locked into mindsets every bit as rigid as before, without a clue as to the particular reason for our new outlook.

Reflection on this baffling behavior can be highly instructive, if our goal is to change someone else's mind. The usual approach to altering another's opinion is to offer a series of linear facts with the expectation that the other person will simply see the validity of the argument and buy into the new way of thinking. Sometimes it works, but, as an overall approach, it is unreliable. Public debates rarely, if ever, result in one side or the other changing its mind. It is not sufficient to simply tell someone that the saliva they spit into a glass should be re-ingested any more than it is to simply send a memo listing the skills necessary to be a good manager. It takes more than pure facts to do the job.

Not surprisingly, when a dramatic shift of mind occurs, the power of the *Aha!* is directly proportional to the rigidity of one's original position. The stronger the belief, the more powerful the mind-changing experience will be. It is a useful metaphor to imagine that to dramatically alter the perception of others requires us each to be the Steven Spielberg in our own movie production. (It is both ironic and appropriate that someone whose name has become synonymous with an all-out assault on the senses would himself be a college dropout.) We may not require quite so many special effects, but the task of altering the perception of others is no less a challenge than moving an audience.

I have four good friends who have survived successive waves of corporate downsizing, in spite of the fact that they do not have college degrees. Their survival is not a mystery to those who are familiar with their accomplishments, however. Their work has a quality to it which makes their competence crystal clear to everyone. If it's your intention to change others' minds about your value to the organization, your actions must speak louder than your words.

Action Steps for Changing Promotional Policy

After years of intense interest, personal experience, and deliberate observation, I can offer the following strategies for combating the negative effects of credentialism. These might be especially useful if you are trying to obtain a promotion in an organization where there is an implied need for credentials that are in fact arbitrary:

1. Find out if there is a written company policy relative to formal education. Sometimes everyone assumes there is when in fact there is not. If the requirement for a degree is only implied, pinning it down can sometimes solve your problem. If not, at least you have a written policy which you can work to change.

2. Are there exceptions to the rule? If so, how many? What is the explanation for the exceptions? Sometimes those at the very top of an organization do not have degrees. How many people in your organization have been promoted despite a lack of paper credentials? It's usually easy to find out, as long as you are discreet about asking.

3. Exactly how many people need to agree before a promotion can be authorized? If you know the attitude of each manager relative to performance and the need for formal credentials, then your strategy for changing their minds will naturally take shape. Often lower-level managers will not consider promoting competent people who are without credentials simply because they believe their boss is against it. Finding out that the boss thinks differently may in and of itself solve the problem. Just asking the question about whether promotion in your organization is based upon credentials or performance will sometimes place the issue in the right context.

4. Realize that in some organizations the implied need for educational credentials may just be a smoke screen covering up the truth—namely, that management has the power to hire and promote anyone they please, anytime they please.

5. Plan the layout and development of your own storyboard production to deliver overwhelming evidence of your ability to rise to the occasion of any likely work situation. (See Portfolio Development.)

The same strategies are also useful in fighting gender bias. All you have to do is use gender as your criterion instead of experience versus educational credentials. The main difference is that, in fighting gender discrimination, you have more regulations to back you up and more tools available for finding remedies. The Equal Employment Opportunity Commission (you can locate them in the federal government section of your local telephone directory) will assist you if you are the victim of gender discrimination.

Once you have accomplished these steps, what needs to be done is fairly easy to assess. If you have minds to change, a good way to broach the subject is to give the people involved some written material such as this book. If you can't get them to read a whole book try for a chapter. If that doesn't work, try for a few pages that specifically address the points you want to make. Maybe you prefer to bring the issue of promotional policy to light without revealing that you're reading a book about proving your own qualifications. That's perfectly understandable. (You can write to Autodidactic Press for a list of extracted passages from this book in essay form, selected for this purpose). Getting everyone's views on the subject of promotions out in the open will often provide the added benefit of putting performance standards that have been somewhat obscure into clear perspective. The next step is to organize all of your resources and to shape, refine, and focus on your purpose.

A strong sense of purpose can be likened to gravity, in that each grain of sand or each drop of water is compelled to do precisely what gravity demands. When our sense of purpose is strong enough, our actions become gravity-like. Your approach to a Me, Inc., posture and the organization of your resources in a way that continually proves you are qualified might take the form of a notebook or a journal with sections or pages for each of the following:

- My objective is:
- My goals are:
- My priorities are:
- My strengths are:
- My aptitudes are:
- My personality type is:
- My learning styles are:
- The trade journals I need to read are:
- The management books I need to read are:
- The Professional associations I should consider joining are:
- Special classes and courses I should take are:
- My skills and accomplishments (see Chapter Six) are documented in:
- The skills and services I possess which others are most likely to want to purchase are:
- My resume confirms my goals and objectives as follows:
- I need to prove my competence to the following people:
- The credentials I still need for qualification are:
- The most practical methods of obtaining them are:
- The future for my skills and special interests is:
- A calendar of special events, peak periods and key dates in my field of expertise is as follows:
- In the future my field of interest is likely to undergo:
- The special dates for my action plans are as follows:

Democracy at Work

My final point is a political caveat concerning the structural changes in our economy that point to the possibility of an end to work as we know it. To assume and maintain a Me, Inc., posture we must each make a continued effort to understand the political context in which we live and work. Today, state of the art management is concerned with "process."[6] Corporations are reengineering themselves which, in many cases, literally means reinventing their organizations from the ground up. Many really are flattening their hierarchies, many are enriching lower level jobs, and many are creating exhilarating opportunities. But all of this exciting renovation is accomplished within a context of power so prevalent it is seldom even noticed. Donald Barlett and James B. Steele make this point in their book *America Who Really Pays the Taxes?*

> In 1954, corporations paid seventy-five cents in taxes for every dollar paid by individuals and families. In 1994, they will pay about twenty cents for every dollar paid by individuals and families. . . .If corporations paid taxes in the 1990s at the same rate they did in the 1950s, nearly two-thirds of the federal deficit would disappear overnight.

In the '50s one wage earner could usually sustain a family. This is far less true today. The preferential tax treatment given major corporations is not a benefit extended to individuals and small businesses. A Me, Inc., business will have to function in this kind of environment without such tax advantages. My point is this: The concept of reengineering businesses, when looked at in detail, seems so logical and so intuitively right that foundational questions of equity never arise. But achieving and sustaining a reasonable quality of life for the vast majority of our citizens (in a global marketplace changing at high velocity) will require that our intellects draw more interest than our bank accounts.

For almost a half-century the U.S. considered the Soviet Union its biggest enemy. During the Cold War, in reaction to propaganda (on both sides), we were conditioned to think that everything private is *good* and everything public is *bad*. The residue of this antagonism is so potent that virtually any proposal that might improve living conditions for those in the lower economic echelons of our society is sure to be branded as socialistic. People use the word socialism daily without a clue as to what it really means. (Socialism exists when the state—in the name of the people—owns the means of production). Ensuring access to the necessities of life for all citizens is not an adjunct bound exclusively to socialism, but is instead a fulfillment of the original purpose for any group of people to band together to form a government in the first place. A growing number of Americans have an obsession with the notion that "some people may get something for nothing," but people who get something for nothing, don't get very much. It would, however, be more productive to worry about the people (or corporations) who get a lot for too little. Such people and businesses gave us the great savings and loan robbery of the 1980s.

Most modern-day Americans have been taught to view tribal life as primitive and therefore inferior to our own. Yet most tribal societies have better met the basic needs for security of all of their members than we have, with far less bellyaching, and without shrill outrage over some members getting something for nothing. It's still true that, in our society, "them that has gets."

We tread closer to socialism when we pool our efforts and resources to wage war than at any other time, and yet we do not refer to soldiers as socialists, nor should we. (And few acknowledge that, in wartime, the poor serve and die in dramatically higher numbers than do those who are higher on the economic ladder). Too few of us realize that the new enemy is what the science of complexity makes clear: unstable markets. Physicists would say, instability is a product of sensitivity to initial conditions, which means there is no way to tell which straw will break the camel's back. Translated to economics, this means Wall Street pundit forecasts are largely based upon illusion.

Economic market systems are inherently unstable, creating a constant threat to everyone who depends upon them. The larger the market, the greater the variables; and the greater the instability, the harder it is to anticipate sensational events. The history of economic depressions suggests they usually arrive when they are least expected. Since we will unhesitatingly go to war to protect our economic interests (the Persian Gulf War is a recent example), the more complex our society becomes, the more dependent we become. The consequences of uncertainty become more threatening for the average citizen. Our extreme dependency masks the interdependence upon which our economy and our political interests are based. Mutual respect is the bedrock of community.

Too many of us seldom acknowledge that government has no lock on bureaucracy. Some of the largest and most flagrant bureaucracies in America are, in fact, private—the American health insurance industry being a case in point. In a democracy, bureaucracy is evidence of shirked responsibility. Bureaucracy claims any service or task which does not sustain enough purpose and commitment to achieve the original goals around which the organization was formed.

Air provides the authority of purpose which gives a balloon its shape. When the air leaks out, efforts to return the balloon to its original form don't work. You can use all sorts of contraptions to expand it, but it will still not look like a balloon is supposed to look. Similarly, citizen participation and involvement provide the air for the balloon of democracy. Simply to howl about how lousy government is, is to blow hot air with no thought to putting it back into the balloon. We get the quality of government and the sort of workplace environment that our democratic efforts warrant.

Thomas Jefferson argued that all laws should expire with each generation so that the full responsibility for government would fall squarely upon the shoulders of every citizen at all times. And yet, most modern-day Americans expect to live their whole lives exempt from involvement in the affairs of government other than to complain about the actions of bureaucrats. When citizens cease to scrutinize, bureaucracy proliferates without regard to whether an organization is public or private. Reengineering is a fancy term for what entrepreneurs on a shoestring budget do all of the time. Bureaucracy moves in and takes over when the employees who follow the entrepreneur are helpless to achieve the original purpose (provided they even know what it was), and in time their own personal interests take over. Thus, meeting the letter of the law and not its intent becomes the dominant agenda.

I use these examples to show that, because of the way we allow our interests to be marginalized by powerful hierarchies, we respond more aggressively to imagined threats than to real ones. Wars *may* occur, but health emergencies are *constant* and *unrelenting*. Such fuzzy thinking is why questions about competence focus on credentials instead of performance.

There is no question that, in a global marketplace, wages have to be competitive, but there are many questions about disparities in compensation at the upper and lower echelons of business organizations. Such questions are only the tip of the iceberg amid issues which veil other inequalities of opportunity that favor big business. Competitiveness is becoming a euphemism for the destruction of a private employer-employee contract.

A competitive society is profoundly dependent upon cooperation. Physicist John H. Holland suggests that "Competition and cooperation may seem antithetical, but at some very deep level, they are two sides of the same coin."[7] Thus, to sustain a society in which all citizens have an opportunity to earn a decent living while engaged in nondestructive employment, is to acknowledge that a tremendous effort is required to minimize the effects of *increasing returns*. Thanks to the nature of high-tech, it's suddenly easy to observe and acknowledge that "them that has gets," and to understand that this advantage has nothing whatsoever to do with efficiency. The QWERTY keyboard is the antithesis of efficiency, yet we can't seem to stop using it. In precisely the same manner, our economic system is rigged, not on the basis of the rights set forth in the Constitution, but on the size of individual pocketbooks. Poor people accused of capital crimes receive legal assistance from harried public defenders barely able to spend more than a couple of hours preparing for their defense. In sharp contrast, consider the legal treatment afforded the rich and famous. Los Angeles County jail authorities considered enlarging their facilities to make room for all of O. J. Simpson's attorneys in the summer of 1994.

To see both work and democracy as *process* might give the appearance that economic justice has finally arrived. But justice in a society taught to associate guilt with lack of achievement is always more readily *apparent than real*, which is why today's workplace has such glaring pay inequities in the first place. It is why corporate executives get rich on salaries, bonuses, and stock options, while employees in lower ranks are barely able to make ends meet. The problem is not the size of the economic pie, but rather who cuts the slices and chooses how the pieces are to be divided. For the sake of appearances, it helps if corporate leaders can get the tax collector to do some of the cutting and slicing for them.

In a nutshell, to be successful in the long term, whether you earn a wage or a fee, your Me, Inc., posture must be kept vibrant by your full participation in the democratic process. Democratic process is the only way to achieve an economic equity that is not totally a product of pyramid power, regardless of whether your dealing with an old corporation or a recently reengineered one.

To stand up for your rights as a citizen today requires a whole new literacy than was necessary for earlier generations. Now, you must understand the political and commercial messages encoded in the media bombarding us daily. At the core of this new literacy is the need to understand the power of hierarchy and the camouflage created by its icons and symbols—all of which help form the very shape of our fundamental beliefs. When more and more people do this, proving we are qualified will be less of a puzzle, because power based upon pretentiousness will be far less tenable. *Them that have will still get*, not because they have a credential, but because they have real skills, progressive values, and the equity afforded by citizenship in America.

End Notes

Introduction

1. Many ineffective college teachers hide behind the argument that research, and not teaching, is the real thrust of their competence and expertise, but in most cases the argument simply doesn't hold water. Nor does this excuse them from depriving students of their expertise by having graduate students teach their classes for them.

Chapter One

1. James R. Fisher. *Work Without Managers*, page 62.
2. Alvin Toffler. *Powershift,* page 74.
3. Philip Slater. *A Dream Deferred*, page 81.
4. Ivan Illich. *Deschooling Society*, page 129.
5. Shelly E. Taylor. *Positive Illusions*. This whole book is a lesson in the self-deceptive nature of human beings.
6. The subtlety with which this is often accomplished is astonishing. Powerful people can pull strings for their offspring and associates without being detected more easily than employers can discriminate against minorities without being caught.
7. Randall Collins. *The Credential Society*, page 17.
8. Ibid., page 174.
9. Charles J. Sikes. *ProfScam*, page 4.
10. Randall Collins. *The Credential Society*, page 198.
11. Ibid., page 5.
12. Alvin Toffler. *Future Shock*, page 273.
13. Peter F. Drucker. *The New Realities*, page 184.
14. Ibid., page 207.
15. Ibid., page 232.
16. Robert M. Pirsig. *Lila*, page 23.
17. Charles Derber, William A. Schwartz, and Yale Magrass. *Power in the Highest Degree*, page 109.
18. Peter F. Drucker. *Post-Capitalist Society*, page 204.

Chapter Two

1. Peter M. Senge. *The Fifth Discipline*, page 82.
2. James R. Fisher. *Work Without Managers*, page 31.
3. Peter F. Drucker. *Post-Capitalist Society*, page 93.
4. Ibid., page 65.
5. Ibid., page 207.
6. James R. Fisher. *Work Without Managers*, page 54.

Chapter Three

1. Robert B. Reich. *The Resurgent Liberal*, pages 91-92.
2. James R. Fisher. *Work Without Managers*, page 31.
3. Robert E. Ornstein. *The Mindfield*, page 44.
4. Tom Peters. *Thriving On Chaos*.
5. James R. Fisher. *Work Without Managers*, page 206.
6. Reinhard Bendix. *Work and Authority in Industry*, page 204.
7. Peter F. Drucker. *The Frontiers of Management*, page 119.
8. Randall Collins. *The Credential Society*, page 15.
9. Ibid., page 15.
10. James R. Fisher. *Work Without Managers*, page 45.
11. Stanley Fish. "Reverse Racism, or How the Pot Got to Call the Kettle Black," *The Atlantic Monthly*, November 1993. The best argument for affirmative action that I have read.
12. James Fallows. *More Like Us*, pages 89, 134.
13. Randall Collins. *The Credential Society*, page 200.

Chapter Four

1. Thomas Gilovich. *How We Know What Isn't So*, page 126.
2. I recently heard a well-known attorney, responsible for overseeing the legal profession, estimate that 25 percent of lawyers practicing law today are incompetent.
3. *The Washington Post*, quoted by Cristine Russell, February 1992.
4. Randall Collins. *The Credential Society*, page 202.
5. Stephen D. Brookfield. *The Skillful Teacher*, page 178.
6. Charles Derber, William A. Schwartz, and Yale Magrass. *Power in the Highest Degree*, page 92.
7. David McClelland. "Testing for Competence Rather Than for Intelligence," *American Psychologist*, January 1973, page 2.
8. David S. Young. *The Rule of Experts*, page 5.
9. Alfie Kohn. *Punished by Rewards*. This book provides a thorough examination of intrinsic and extrinsic motivation.
10. James R. Fisher. *Work Without Managers*, page 224.
11. David McClelland. "Testing for Competence Rather Than for Intelligence," *American Psychologist*, January 1973, page 2.
12. Ibid., page 7.

Chapter Five

1. Philip Slater. *A Dream Deferred*, page 12.
2. Ivar Berg. *Education and Jobs*, page 85.
3. Thomas Gilovich. *How We Know What Isn't So*, page 65.
4. James Fallows. *More Like Us*, page 157.
5. Benjamin DeMott. *The Imperial Middle*, pages 130-131.
6. Laurence G. Boldt. *Zen and the Art of Making a Living*, page 10.

Chapter Six

1. Richard N. Bolles. *What Color is Your Parachute?*, page 51.
2. Ellen J. Langer. *Mindfulness*, page 47.
3. Henry David Thoreau. *The Portable Thoreau*, Carl Bode, ed., page 260.
4. Ivar Berg. *Education and Jobs*, pages 162-175.
5. Charles D. Hayes. *Self-University*, page 199. Section 3308 of Title 5, United States Code, provides that no minimum educational requirements will be prescribed in any civil service examination except for such scientific, technical, or professional positions the duties of which the Office of Personnel Management decides cannot be performed by a person who does not have this education. Section 3308 also provides that OPM will make its reasons for these decisions a part of public record. This restriction includes all formal schooling whether at grade school, high school or college level.
6. This related phenomenon is easily observable and is, in fact, partly responsible for the policy of tenure in colleges and universities. You may have observed, for example, that radical opinions have a way of surfacing when and only when professors cannot be fired.
7. Randall Collins. *The Credential Society*, page 16.
8. Jerry L. Wight. "The New Age of Higher Education in America." (Unpublished paper, 1993.)
9. Huey B. Long. *Adult and Continuing Education*, page 186.

Chapter Seven

1. What is not so clear is how this metaphor, "artificial intelligence" on the horizon, and the biotechnical sciences are going to influence our deeply held beliefs about the way we view the world. The mechanistic model of the industrial age is dying, but what kind of a world view will take its place is still to be determined.
2. Shoshana Zuboff. *In the Age of the Smart Machine*, pages 58-96.
3. Ibid., page 40.
4. Ibid., pages 62-82.
5. Ibid., pages 75-76.
6. M. Mitchell Waldrop. *Complexity*, pages 17-35.
7. Ibid., page 17.
8. William Bridges. *Jobshift*, page 138.
9. Jeremy Rifkin. *Time Wars*, page 192.
10. Ibid., page 102.
11. Ibid., page 124.
12. W. Lambert Gardiner. *The Ubiquitous Chip*.
13. No matter how hard one tries to be objective in making this type of prediction, one can usually find traces of hope or wishful thinking. My statement is no exception. Still, I think there are many compelling reasons why a philosophy reminiscent of Ralph Waldo Emerson is a distinct possibility: First, society and culture are changing faster than at any time in history, and we know from practical experience that rapid change produces a strong need for belief, something to cling to, some type of refuge to ride out the storm of change. An openness toward

knowledge, as in Emerson's Transcendentalism, offers much more in the way of emotional security than rigid fundamentalist dogma or the rise in Shirley Mclaineisms.

Second, millions of babyboomers will have reached the life-stage of realizing their own mortality. When you combine these two trends, with the hangover of excess from the 1980s and the fact that millions of middle-class, middle managers (people who always provided the sheet music for the tune of the American Dream) have found themselves downsized or laid off through corporate restructuring, the dissonance necessary for reevaluating values and priorities will be profound. I believe this is why there is a very subtle but certain groundswell of Emersonian and Thoreauvian-like quotations creeping into more and more contemporary books. As we approach the Third Millennium there will a tidal wave of dissonance.

14. Ronald L. Krannich. *Careering and Re-careering for the 1990's*, page xv.
15. Robert M. Pirsig. *Zen and the Art of Motorcycle Maintenance*, page ix.
16. Donald L. Bartlett and James B. Steele. *America What Went Wrong?*, page ix.
17. Ivar Berg. *Education and Jobs*, page 191.

Chapter Eight

1. Richard Saul Wurman. *Information Anxiety*, page 195.
2. Peter M. Senge. *The Fifth Discipline*, page 211.
3. John Naisbitt. *Global Paradox*, page 12.
4. Ivan Illich. *The Right To Useful Employment*, page 40.
5. Ibid., page 46.
6. Michael Hammer and James Champy. *Reengineering the Corporation*, page 35.
7. John H. Holland as quoted in *Complexity*, by M. Mitchell Waldrop, page 185.

Recommended Reading

Credentialism

Berg, Ivar. *Education and Jobs: The Great Training Robbery*. New York: Praeger Publishers, 1970.

Collins, Randall. *The Credential Society*. New York: Academic Press, 1979.

Derber, Charles, with William A. Schwartz and Yale Magrass. *Power in the Highest Degree: Professionals and the Rise of the New Mandarin Order*. New York: Oxford University Press, 1990.

Dore, Ronald. *The Diploma Disease*. Berkeley, CA: University of California Press, 1976.

Fallows, James. "The Case Against Credentialing." *The Atlantic Monthly*, December 1985, pp. 49-67.

Illich, Ivan. *Deschooling Society*. New York: Harper Colophon Books, 1971.

Illich, Ivan. *The Right to Useful Employment*. London: Marion Boyars, 1978.

McClelland, D.C. *The Achieving Society*. Princeton, NJ: D. Van Nostrand, 1961.

Sikes, Charles J. *Profscam: Professors and the Demise of Higher Education*. New York: St. Martin's Press, 1988.

Young, David S. *The Rule of Experts*. Washington, DC: Cato Institute, 1987.

Education and Educational Resources

Bear, John. *Bear's Guide to Earning College Degrees Non-traditionally*. Berkely: Ten Speed Press 1995.

Bird, Caroline. *The Case Against College*. New York: David McKay Co., 1975.

Brookfield, Stephen D. *The Skillful Teacher*. San Francisco: Jossey-Bass, 1990.

Draves, Bill. *The Free University: A Model for Lifelong Learning*. Chicago: Association Press, 1980.

Gardner, Howard. *Frames of Mind*. New York: Basic Books, 1983.

Gross, Ronald. *The Independent Scholar's Handbook*. Berkely: Ten Speed Press, 1993.

Gross, Ronald. *Peak Learning*. Los Angeles: Jeremy P. Tarcher, 1991.

Knowles, Malcolm S. *Self-Directed Learning: A Guide for Learners and Teachers*. New York: The Adult Education Co., 1975.

Kozol, Jonathan. *Illiterate America*. Garden City, NY: Anchor Press/Doubleday, 1985.

Long, Huey B. *Adult and Continuing Education*. New York: Teachers College Press, 1983.

Morgan, Edward P. *Inequality in Classroom Learning: Schooling and Democratic Citizenship*. New York: Praeger Publishers, 1977.

Owen, David. *None of the Above: Behind the Myth of Scholastic Aptitude*. Boston: Houghton Mifflin, 1986.

Postman, Neil, and Charles Weingarten. *Teaching as a Subversive Activity*. New York: Dell, 1969.

Smith, Page. *Killing the Spirit*. New York: Penguin Books, 1990.

Whitlock, Baird W. *Educational Myths I Have Known and Loved*. New York: Schocken Books, 1986.

General Interest

Anderson, Walter Truett. *Reality Isn't What It Used To Be*. San Francisco: Harper & Row, 1990.

Barlett, Donald L., and James B. Steele. *America What Went Wrong?* Kansas City, MO: Andrews & McMeel, 1992.

Barlett, Donald L., and James B. Steele. *America Who Really Pays the Taxes?* Kansas City, MO: Andrews & McMeel, 1994.

Davis, Stanley M. *Future Perfect.* Reading, MA: Addison-Wesley, 1987.

DeMott, Benjamin. *The Imperial Middle.* New York: William Morrow & Co., 1990.

Emerson, Ralph Waldo. *The Portable Emerson.* Edited by Carl Bode. New York: Penguin Books, 1981

Fallows, James. *More Like Us: Making America Great Again.* Boston: Houghton Mifflin, 1989.

Festinger, Leon. *A Theory of Cognitive Dissonance.* Stanford, CA: Stanford University Press, 1962.

Fish, Stanley. "Reverse Racism, or How the Pot Got to Call the Kettle Black." *The Atlantic Monthly*, November 1993.

Gardiner, W. Lambert. *The Ubiquitous Chip: The Human Impact of Electronic Technology.* Quebec Canada: Scot & Siliclone, 1987.

Gilovich, Thomas. *How We Know What Isn't So: The Fallibility of Human Reason in Everyday Life.* New York: Macmillan, 1991.

Gould, Stephen Jay. *Ever Since Darwin.* New York: W. W. Norton, 1977.

Gould, Stephen Jay. *The Mismeasure of Man.* New York: W. W. Norton, 1981.

Hyatt, Carole, and Linda Gottlieb. *When Smart People Fail.* New York: Simon & Schuster, 1987.

Kanter, Donald L., and Philip H. Mirvis. *The Cynical Americans: Living and Working in an Age of Discontent and Disillusion.* San Francisco: Jossey-Bass, 1989.

Kanter, R. M. *Men and Women of the Corporation.* New York: Basic Books, 1977.

Katen, Thomas Ellis. *Doing Philosophy.* Englewood Cliffs, NJ: Prentice-Hall, 1973.

Keiser, T. W., and J. L. Keiser. *The Anatomy of Illusion.* Springfield, IL: Charles C. Thomas, 1987.

Kelley, Robert E. *The Gold-Collar Worker: Harnessing the Brain Power of the New Work Force.* Reading, MA: Addison-Wesley, 1985.

Kemp, Nigel. *Information Technology and People: Designing for the Future.* Cambridge, MA: MIT Press, 1987.

Kohn, Alfie. *No Contest: The Case Against Competition.* Boston: Houghton Mifflin, 1986.

Kohn, Alfie. *The Brighter Side of Human Nature.* New York: Basic Books, 1990.

Langer, Ellen J. *Mindfulness.* New York: Addison-Wesley, 1989.

Lapham, Lewis H. *The Wish For Kings.* New York: Grove Press, 1993.

Martel, Leon. *Mastering Change: The Key to Business Success.* New York: Simon & Schuster, 1986.

Miller, Arthur G., ed. *In the Eye of the Beholder: Contemporary Issues in Stereotyping.* New York: Praeger Publishers, 1982.

Naisbitt, John. *Global Paradox.* New York: William Morrow & Co., 1994.

Ornstein, Robert E. *The Mindfield.* New York: Grossman Publishers, 1976.

Pascarella, Perry. *The New Achievers: Creating a Modern Work Ethic.* New York: The Free Press, 1984.

Piirto, Rebecca. *Beyond Mind Games.* New York: American Demographics Books, 1991.

Pirsig, Robert M. *Zen and the Art of Motorcycle Maintenance: An Inquiry into Values.* New York: Bantam Books, 1985.

Pirsig, Robert M. *Lila: An Inquiry into Morals.* New York: Bantam Books, 1991.

Raelin, Joseph A. *The Clash of Cultures.* Boston: Harvard Business School Press, 1985.

Reich, Robert B. *The Resurgent Liberal (and Other Unfashionable Prophecies).* New York: Time Books, 1989.

Rifkin, Jeremy. *Time Wars.* New York: Henry Holt, 1987.

Rifkin, Jeremy. *The End of Work.* New York: Tarcher/Putnam, 1995.

Roszak, Theodore. *The Cult of Information: The Folklore of Computers and the True Art of Thinking.* New York: Pantheon Books, 1986.

Sartre, Jean Paul. *Being and Nothingness.* Translated by H. Barnes. New York: Philosophical Library, 1956.

Slater, Philip. *Earthwalk.* New York: E. P. Dutton, 1974.

Slater, Philip. *Wealth Addiction.* New York: E. P. Dutton, 1980.

Slater, Philip. *A Dream Deferred.* Boston, MA: Beacon Press Books, 1991.

Smith, Huston. *The Religions of Man.* New York: Harper & Row, 1986.

Sternberg, Robert J. *Beyond IQ: A Triarchic Theory of Human Intelligence.* Cambridge: Cambridge University Press, 1985.

Sternberg, Robert J. *The Triarchic Mind: A New Theory of Human Intelligence.* New York: Viking Penguin, 1988.

Taylor, Shelly E. *Positive Illusions.* New York: Basic Books, 1989.

Thoreau, Henry David. Edited by Carl Bode. *The Portable Thoreau.* New York: Viking Penguin, 1947.

Toffler, Alvin. *Future Shock.* New York: Bantam Books, 1971.

Toffler, Alvin. *Powershift: Knowledge, Wealth, and Violence at the Edge of the 21st Century.* New York: Bantam Books, 1990.

Waldrop, M. Mitchell. *Complexity.* New York: Simon & Schuster, 1992.

Management

Bendix, Reinhard. *Work and Authority in Industry.* Berkeley, CA: University of California Press, 1974.

Bardwick, Judith M. *Danger in the Comfort Zone.* New York: AMACOM, 1991.

Deming, W. Edwards. *Out of the Crisis.* Cambridge, MA: MIT Press, 1986.

De Pree, Max. *Leadership is an Art.* New York: Dell Publishing, 1989.

Drucker, Peter F. *Toward the Next Economics and Other Essays.* New York: Harper & Row, 1981.

Drucker, Peter F. *Innovation and Entrepreneurship: Practice and Principles.* New York: Harper & Row, 1985.

Drucker, Peter F. *The Frontiers of Management: Where Tomorrow's Decisions Are Being Shaped Today.* New York: Truman Talley Books/E. P. Dutton, 1986.

Drucker, Peter F. *The New Realities: In Government and Politics/ In Economics and Business/ In Society and World View.* New York: Harper & Row, 1989.

Drucker, Peter F. *Managing for the Future: The 1990s and Beyond.* New York: Truman Talley Books/Dutton, 1992.

Drucker, Peter F. *Post-Capitalist Society.* New York: HarperCollins, 1993.

Fisher, James R. Jr. *Work Without Managers*. Tampa: The Delta Group, 1991.

Garson, Barbara. *The Electronic Sweatshop*. New York: Penguin Books, 1989.

Hammer, Michael, and James Champy. *Reengineering the Corporation*. New York: HarperBusiness, 1993.

Handy, Charles. *The Age of Unreason*. Boston MA: Harvard Business School Press, 1989.

Handy, Charles. *The Age of Paradox*. Boston MA: Harvard Business School Press, 1994.

Naisbitt, John, and Patricia Aburdene. *Re-Inventing the Corporation*. New York: Warner Books, 1985.

Pinchot, Gifford, and Elizabeth Pinchot. *The End of Bureaucracy & the Rise of the Intelligent Organization*. San Francisco: Berrett-Koehler, 1994.

Peters, Tom. *Thriving on Chaos: Handbook for a Management Revolution*. New York: Alfred A. Knopf, 1987.

Peters, Tom. *Liberation Management*. New York: Alfred A. Knopf, 1992.

Peters, Tom, and Nancy Austin. *A Passion for Excellence: The Leadership Difference*. New York: Random House, 1985.

Shorris, Earl. *The Oppressed Middle: Politics of Middle Management, Scenes from Corporate Life*. New York: Anchor Press, 1981.

Zuboff, Shoshana. *In the Age of the Smart Machine*. New York: Basic Books, 1988.

Self-Education, Career and Self-Development

Benziger, I. Katherine, and Anne Sohn. *The Art of Using Your Whole Brain*. Rockwell, TX: Benziger Publishing Co., 1989.

Boldt, Laurence G. *Zen and the Art of Making a Living*. New York: Penguin Books, 1991.

Bolles, Richard N. *The Three Boxes of Life: And How to Get Out of Them*. Berkeley, CA: Ten Speed Press, 1981.

Bolles, Richard N. *What Color Is Your Parachute?* Berkeley, CA: Ten Speed Press, 1992.

Bridges, William. *Jobshift: How to Prosper in a Workplace Without Jobs*. New York: Addison-Wesley, 1994.

Covey, Stephen R. *The Seven Habits of Highly Effective People*. New York: Simon & Shuster, 1989.

De Bono, Edward. *De Bono's Thinking Course*. New York: Facts on File Publications, 1982.

Druckman, Daniel, and Robert A. Bjork, eds. *In the Mind's Eye: Enhancing Human Performance*. Washington, D.C., National Academy Press, 1991.

Garfield, Charles. *Peak Performers: The New Heroes of American Business*. New York: William Morrow, 1986.

Hakim, Cliff. *We Are All Self-Employed: The New Social Contract in a Changed World*. San Francisco: Berrett-Koehler, 1994.

Hayes, Charles D. *Self-University: The Price of Tuition Is the Desire to Learn. Your Degree Is a Better Life*. Wasilla, AK: Autodidactic Press, 1989.

Hayes, Charles D. *Beyond the American Dream: Finding Purpose and Meaning on the Other Side of Culture*. (Forthcoming.)

Hayes, Charles D. *Lifelong Learning Versus Belief in a Postmodern World*. (Forthcoming.)

Herrman, Ned. *The Creative Brain*. Lake Lure, NC: Ned Herrman/Brain Books, 1989.

Hooker, Judith, and Dick Teresi. *The Three Pound Universe*. New York: Dell Publishing Company, 1987.

Hutchison, Michael. *Megabrain: New Tools and Techniques for Brain Growth and Mind Expansion*. New York: William Morrow, 1986.

Kinder, Melvyn. *Going Nowhere Fast*. New York: Prentice-Hall Press, 1990.

Knowles, Malcolm S. *The Modern Practice of Adult Education: From Pedagogy to Andragogy*. Chicago: Follett, 1980.

Kohl, Herbert. *The Question Is College*. New York: Random House, 1989.

Kohn, Alfie. *Punished by Rewards*. New York: Houghton Mifflin, 1993

Krannich, Ronald L. *Careering and Re-careering for the 1990's*. Manassas, VA: Impact Publications, 1989.

Meiland, Jack W. *College Thinking*. New York: New American Library, 1981.

Riso, Don R. *Personality Types: Using the Enneagram for Self-Discovery*. Boston: Houghton Mifflin, 1987.

Schaffer, William A. *Hi-Tech Jobs for Lo-Tech People*. New York: American Management Association, 1994.

Schank, Roger, and Peter Childers. *The Creative Attitude*. New York: Macmillan, 1988.

Senge, Peter M. *The Fifth Discipline: The Art and Practice of the Learning Organization*. New York: Doubleday/Currency, 1990.

Simosko, Susan. *Earn College Credit for What You Know*. Washington, DC: Acropolis Books, 1985.

Sinetar, Marsha. *Do What You Love, the Money Will Follow: Discovering Your Right Livelihood*. New York: Paulist Press, 1987.

Sinetar, Marsha. *Elegant Choices, Healing Choices*. New York: Paulist Press, 1988.

Smith, Deborahann. *Temp: How to Survive and Thrive in the World of Temporary Employment*. Boston: Shambhala, 1994.

Stumpf, Stephen A., and Joel R. DeLuca. *Learning to Use What You Already Know*. San Francisco: Berrett-Koehler, 1994.

Tannen, Deborah. *You Just Don't Understand*. New York: William Morrow, 1990.

Wurman, Richard Saul. *Information Anxiety*. New York: Bantam Books, 1989.

Index

ability, 3, 9, 36, 40, 48-50, 60, 65-70, 81, 87, 90-92, 101, 105, 117, 119, 121, 124-127, 147
academic freedom, 11
achievement, merit and, 9
affirmative action, 59-60
aptitude, 7, 10, 68-69, 79, 87, 102, 112, 137, 148
associations, professional, 63, 65
automation and control, 48; computer, 49

babyboomers, 123
Bardwick, Judith M., *Danger in the Comfort Zone*, 45
Barlett, Donald and James B. Steele, *America Who Really Pays the Taxes?*, 148-149
Bear, John, *Bear's Guide to Earning College Degrees Non-traditionally*, 112
behavior, understanding human, 14
Benziger, Katherine and Anne Sohn, *The Art of Using Your Whole Brain*, 97, 101
Berg, Ivar, *Education and Jobs*, 79, 100, 129
biotechnologies, 129
Bird, Caroline, *The Case Against College*, 72-73
Boldt, Laurence G., *Zen and the Art of Making a Living*, 90, 101
Bolles, Richard Nelson, *What Color is Your Parachute?*, 9, 97, 101
brain hemispheres (*see* whole brain theory)
Bridges, William, *Jobshift*, 120, 131, 143
Brookfield, Stephen D., *The Skillful Teacher*, 65
bureaucracy, 78, 84, 100; Federal, 100
Bush, George, 84, 91

careers, preparation, 21; advancement, 60; changing, 126;

search strategies, 126
caste system, 7
certification, 67-68
Challenger space shuttle, 28, 30
change, 123-124; nature of, 116
chaos, future of, 127
cheating, 71
Chernobyl, 28
civil service, 100
classlessness, 87
colleges, attendance and success, 67; and universities, 78, 85, 107; traditional and nontraditional, 106-107, 109
Collins, Randall, *The Credential Society*, 16, 20, 21, 57
communication skills, 90, 91, 129
competence, 2, 36, 80, 81, 82, 90, 98
contract employment, 39-40
cultural capital, 11-12
cyclical change, 116
credentials, 15, 18, 22, 24, 75, 78, 81, 100, 131, 133-134; educational, 3-4, 17, 33, 55; currency of, 8; schooling and, 9, 23; degrees, 66; fraudulent, 87; entitlement, 86
Crouse, James, 70
cultural expectations, 99
curricula, 8, 77

Darwin, Charles, 71
decredentialing society, 20, 21
DeMott, Benjamin, *The Imperial Middle*, 87
DePree, Max, *Leadership is an Art*, 51
degree, 72-73, 79, 90; doctorate, 83; nontraditional, 112; external, 112
Derber, Charles and William A. Schwartz, and Yale Magrass, *Power in the Highest Degree*, 19, 13-14, 66
Dore, Ronald, *The Diploma Disease*, 77
downsizing, 37-38, 40, 51, 61, 73, 128-129, 131, 133, 146

Order Information

Quantity	Description	Price	Total
	Proving You're Qualified:. Strategies for Competent People Without College Degrees. (paperback)	**$16.95**	$
	Self-University: The Price of Tuition Is the Desire to Learn Your Degree Is a Better Life. (hardcover).	**$24.95**	
	Self-University Newsletter, published quarterly (One year).	**$20.00**	
	Two years.	**$35.00**	
	Decredentialing Society (This is material excerpted from *Proving You're Qualified* in an 8 1/2 x 11 essay format for the purpose of roundtable discussion. Permission is granted to make copies for this purpose only.)	**$12.00**	
	Shipping & Handling (First book: $3, each additional book: $1. Newsletter and Essay shipped postage paid.)	$	
		TOTAL:	$

Mail To:
Autodidactic Press
P.O. Box 872749
Wasilla, AK 99687

Credit Card Orders
(books only)
Call 1-800-247-6553